Ken McGRATH
HAND ON HEART

KT-374-255

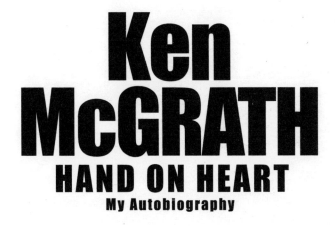

Ken McGrath
HAND ON HEART
My Autobiography

Ken McGrath

with Michael Moynihan

BLACK & WHITE PUBLISHING

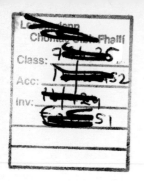

First published 2016
by Black & White Publishing Ltd
29 Ocean Drive, Edinburgh EH6 6JL

1 3 5 7 9 10 8 6 4 2   16 17 18 19

ISBN: 978 1 78530 075 2

Copyright © Ken McGrath and Michael Moynihan 2016

The right of Ken McGrath and Michael Moynihan
to be identified as the authors of this work has
been asserted by them in accordance with the
Copyright, Designs and Patents Act 1988.

All rights reserved.
No part of this publication may be reproduced,
stored in a retrieval system, or transmitted in any form,
or by any means, electronic, mechanical, photocopying,
recording or otherwise, without permission in
writing from the publisher.

The publisher has made every reasonable effort
to contact copyright holders of images in this book.
Any errors are inadvertent and anyone who for
any reason has not been contacted is invited to write
to the publisher so that a full acknowledgment
can be made in subsequent editions of this work.

A CIP catalogue record for this book is available from the British Library.

Typeset by Iolaire, Newtonmore
Printed in Great Britain by Clays Ltd, St Ives plc

CONTENTS

ACKNOWLEDGEMENTS

Thanks to all the people who made my story readable and enjoyable (I hope). I never thought I'd ever write a book about my life, and I've tried to be as open and honest as I could.

First I want to thank my parents, Pat and Ann. They've raised five kids who understand what it means to be a family, and we appreciate all the sacrifices they made; they've always wanted the best for us.

To Roy, Eoin, Pat and Lorna – thanks for always being there. We have a great relationship with each other, rooted in the crack we had with each other growing up, and which we still have today.

Huge thanks to my earliest hurling mentors in Mount Sion – Paddy Sheridan, Jim Hennessy, John Meaney Sr and two great hurling men from the school, Brother Griffey and Brother Dowling. They made learning our trade very easy but also, and more important, very enjoyable.

Huge thanks also to all the lads I played with for Mount Sion. We had brilliant times, great crack and huge success – you couldn't put into words what Mount Sion has meant to me (though I've tried here!) If only we could rewind time . . .

My only dream as a child was to wear the Waterford jersey. To do that for fifteen years was unbelievable. To all the men who I shared the dressing room with – simply put, we had the time of our lives. Thanks, lads.

My thanks also to Tony Mansfield, Gerald McCarthy, Justin McCarthy and Davy Fitzgerald and all their selectors and trainers. Every one of them in their own way had a huge influence on our journey.

Thanks also to my brother Eoin in particular for being a great boss: Mean Bean Coffee Co. is a great place to work and I love it there.

Thanks to Michael Moynihan for all his help (and to Marjorie, Clara, Bridget, Bobby and Breda for helping him to help me). Plenty of cake was harmed in the making of this book.

A special mention for Eddie O'Donnell, the busiest retired person I know: thanks for everything, Eddie.

To all the gang at Black and White – Campbell, Ali, Chris, Daiden, everybody – you've made it a hugely enjoyable experience. Thanks also to Simon and Declan at Gill Hess for making everything run so smoothly.

To the Waterford supporters: we've been through a roller coaster of emotion over the years, but you've always been brilliant to me and I respect that. Forever.

Finally, to Dawn, Ceilin, Ali and Izzy – you mean everything to me and I can't wait for our journey to continue.

INTRODUCTION

It's never a good sign when they draw the curtain around your hospital bed.

It was about half past seven on a Friday evening in the hospital, and I was sitting on the bed chatting to Dawn when the doctors came in.

I'd just spent two whole days being wheeled from pillar to post, getting tests and tests after tests and, to be honest, I was terrified when I saw the group of doctors approach the bed and surround us.

I'd had blood tests, ECO tests, CT scans, you name it. I didn't mind, particularly, because I wanted to get to the bottom of whatever it was that was making me so sick, and I was in a part of the hospital called the MAU, where you're basically treated as a lab rat with everything being examined.

The basic problem was that nobody knew what was wrong with me. I'd had every test you could think of and a few I'd never imagined, but there were no answers. The first sentence I heard when they pulled the curtain around, though, was ominous enough.

'You're going to have a long stay here.'

I looked up at them and said, 'Fair enough, but I have training on Tuesday night.'

One of the female doctors said, 'No, we're talking about a long stay here – a minimum of six weeks at least.'

That was a fair shock to get. They went on to say that they'd found the problem, or they were almost one hundred per cent sure they had, but I was still trying to get my head around the six-week stay I was facing.

At that stage I was hoping that they'd find something, as I'd been out of sorts for far too long. I knew I wasn't right.

What I wasn't anticipating was what was really ahead of me: a stay of nearly three months in hospital, ending with my chest being sawed open and a valve in my heart getting replaced.

———

1

Hillview: Growing Up in Waterford

I'm Waterford born and bred. My mother and father are both from the city, a part everyone in Waterford would know as the top of the town. Dad is from Tycor Avenue, just behind Walsh Park, near the jute factory – it closed down years ago, but it's what people in Waterford would still call the building.

My father's dad, Jack, worked in the jute factory when it was a going concern, though he was in America for years before that. I never met him – he died before I was born – but I knew Lizzie, my granny, well. A character.

My father, Pat, has eight sisters and a brother – Jockser – and he's the youngest. There were nine of them in the house growing up. Normal enough numbers for back then.

My mother, Ann, is from St John's Park in Waterford, out by Kilcohan Park. When she was growing up it would have been almost out in the country, but it's been swallowed up by the city since. She had three brothers, though one, Brian, passed away at the age of ten, and two sisters.

My parents have been together since they were fifteen, which was the same year Dad went into Waterford Crystal to serve his time as an apprentice before, in time, becoming a glass cutter.

The way they tell it they spent most of their time before getting married out walking – walking around town, out in the country, him walking her home and then walking home himself. Good for the fitness.

They got married at twenty-one, in 1974, and moved to Hillview, a new estate then. No moving in together before getting married back then, and they're still there. Number 12, a normal three-bed semi. It's about five hundred yards from Mount Sion club, though some of the houses on the estate back onto the club grounds.

My earliest memory is of the street. At that time there seemed to be one car to a house, if that, and a lot of the housewives didn't seem to drive, so in the morning all the fathers would get in the cars and head for work – a lot of them heading to the glass, as Waterford Crystal was known – and the street was very quiet until they'd come home.

We were out on the street playing as kids very early as a result. Me, Shane Twomey (or Trigger), Gavin Foley (or Growler), Jamie O'Meara (or Moose) – we'd all still be friends, having started off as kids playing soccer on the road.

You're talking about the early eighties onwards, so computer games weren't an attraction, though in fairness, one of the lads on the street, Jas Power, had a computer, and it had a game – 'Emlyn Hughes', which dates it nicely.

It took about thirty minutes to load, we'd go up to his room and hang around for ages to get a turn . . . we usually went back out onto the road playing around. Because cars were so scarce we'd have the full use of the road – two garages for goals, then a game of four-on-four, or six-on-six.

Soccer was the usual game – all you need is a ball, after all – but there was tennis when Wimbledon was on, hurling, cricket . . . anything that was going on we copied out on the road. If the Italian soccer was on television we'd watch it and then pile out of the houses to imitate van Basten or Baresi or whoever else we'd seen as soon as the credits rolled.

Jamie O'Meara, Moose, ended up going to America one summer and brought back a baseball bat and glove, so we even played a World Series in Hillview. Every sport welcome.

The big difference then was the absence of cars, even though it's not that long ago. Nowadays we often head up to my parents' house on a Friday evening – my mother throws on a huge lunch, we're all there chatting, it's great.

But we'd account for four or five cars rolling up. Every house has two cars in front of it, at least. There are evenings you can barely get up the road at all, so the chances of kids being able to get out and play a game of four-on-four are pretty slim.

In our time you'd hear a car slowing down out on the main road to turn into Hillview, so you could pick up the ball until it passed; we often played a full game, start to finish, without interruption.

Roy, my brother, was the leader. Always. He was a couple of years older so he tended to take charge, and to take charge of the rules. If it was the fortnight of Wimbledon and he was Boris Becker, then there were no balls that went out. His always landed inside the line.

It was all sport, really. On a summer evening you'd be out on the street until ten o'clock: you'd only go in when it was dark. There might be five or six different groups of kids of different ages, playing or chatting or chasing around until it got too dark to see and you were called in.

It was safe. That was the crucial thing. No one worried about kids being out at that hour of night – you were a few yards from your front door, what could happen?

There were green areas all around us. At that time Hillview was on the edge of town, and even though the city has spread past it now there's still plenty of green around it.

There are two years between us – Roy is the oldest, then there are two years to me, then two years to Eoin, two years to Pat and two years to Lorna.

Roy is the leader. I'd have hung around as a child with him rather than Eoin, and he was the best at everything as a kid – in cycling he was Sean Kelly, in tennis he was Boris Becker. All of that. I was best man at his wedding and all the speeches focused on that, him leading the way. The boss.

He was the first to go to secondary, first to play Tony Forristal, first to win a county medal, first to play senior for Mount Sion – a fiery wing-back.

He probably lacked a tiny bit of pace and size for senior intercounty, but he was our mainstay all the way up at underage level; he was always the key man. At senior he was midfield, a huge part of the team and a typical club player in that some people might underestimate him, and find out a little too late that they'd made a bad mistake.

He marked them all for ten years, every top midfielder. Tough as nails. In the 2002 Munster club final against Sixmilebridge in Thurles he met John Reddan with a shoulder, and Reddan – who was six two and built – slid down to him. Reddan got his handpass away to Christy Chaplin, in fairness, and Chaplin equalised from the pass to make the game level, but I don't remember Reddan contributing after that. Roy mastered that art, of giving shoulders, and he was a huge presence for us for years in the middle of the field.

(The fact that he has seven county medals, and Eoin and I have only the six, gives him that to hold over us, too.)

Roy's a financial adviser with Fitzgerald Insurance: first of us to go to college and get a degree, good to study. He was on the Waterford RTC team that won the Fitzgibbon in 1994, so he always showed the way.

For instance, he was the first of us to go abroad – to Scotland on a school trip – and, in fairness, he brought back a Dundee United jersey for me, which I wore for years.

He's a real oldest brother in that way, leading the way and giving the good example, but he has his mad side too. He sang for years in a band, The Remedies, at weddings and in pubs; we'd often play a huge game and he'd go off after, play a gig in the Kaz Bar or Muldoon's and come back up to us in Mount Sion afterwards to celebrate the win.

We're great pals now but it was the usual brother-on-brother warfare as kids. He'd hit me and I'd go after him with a hurley, or chase him up the stairs with the poker (his pace was top class then).

But we looked up to him, and he always delivered on anything he put his mind to.

Eoin was the same as a kid as he is now. A ball of energy which never stopped. Ever.

He can't relax, it's all go – being in the coffee business suits him – and he can't sit still for a minute (my own daughter Ali is similar; she can't relax either).

As a kid I don't know how many days out or trips he held up because we'd be trying to find him, and even when he turned up it wasn't all plain sailing. We were on our way up to Clonmel one time and he wasn't talking properly, so the car stopped for investigations.

It turned out he'd been chewing on an old log-box and had carved a hole in his tongue, so off to the hospital: four stitches.

Another time – again in Clonmel – he fell off a picnic table and split his head open. Another four or five stitches. Always something.

Yet another outing, with all the cousins on my father's side up into the mountains, he fell again. This time he had to get sixteen stitches in his leg. Family day out ruined. Everyone home. Eoin in the hospital. The usual.

The best of all, though, was when Lorna was born. My father brought us all out and about and Eoin decided to take a walk along the bandstand in the park: took a header off it and destroyed himself.

We ended up going to the hospital to get him stitched – my mother's in labour, remember – and I stayed out in the car while they brought him in. I was bored, I had a small cowboy hat to play with – a very small hat – and out of curiosity I decided to see if it would fit up my nose . . .

I had to stroll into the hospital, pointing at my nose, where the hat was jammed; Eoin was getting even more stitches sewn into his head; and my mother was having a baby.

Busy times.

Nothing would faze him, though. He was hardy out. He and his buddies were younger than us and wanted to hang around with us. The couple of years makes a big difference to kids, of course, and we didn't want them anywhere near us, and then they'd get into scrapes.

When he got to twelve or so he'd play for the team I was on, though he was two years younger than us; there was no need to mind him, the tough little blond kid speeding around.

Pat was in Australia for five years – the golden child of the family, as everyone says. We were all in the middle of the worst recession in decades here while he was away, but my mother was telling us about poor Pat and his problems down under: 'Poor Pat, it was thirty degrees in Australia today.'

He's quieter than Eoin and Roy, probably more like me, and because he was that bit younger he'd have hung around with his own gang.

But he got into trouble himself the odd time as well. My parents extended the kitchen of the house in 1986, and in winter that became our playground when we couldn't play outside.

My mother had a part-time job and when my father was dropping her over to it, he'd tell us, 'Not in that kitchen.'

As soon as they were out the door the games started. Roy might be bowling in a cricket game in the kitchen and Eoin letting fly as though he were in Lord's, scattering Waterford Crystal and cups everywhere. Full sliding tackles in soccer games there, banging your toes off the radiator.

(My father would come back and say, 'I hope ye weren't

out there in the kitchen,' and the four of us would be sweating from the effort, perched in a row on the couch: 'Nah, we never moved from here.')

But one evening we were holding the Olympics out in the kitchen, and Pat was aiming for a gold medal in the long jump, so he hopped up on the press and leaned back through the window for leverage – only to smash out through the window, onto the drive.

He could have been killed, of course, but we ended up laughing. When my father asked us what happened, we just sang dumb: 'No idea.'

Four young fellas in a house? What would you expect?

Lorna was born in 1985. She's the youngest. The baby. The pet. Hers are the kids Granny and Granddad mind all the time.

She was a tomboy – probably had to be, the house she was in – but very quiet. The teacher came to the house when she started school, wanting to know why she wouldn't say 'anseo'. It wasn't that she couldn't, she just didn't want to speak.

She got roped into all our games – in the slip if we were playing cricket, a handy gig unless Roy saw her missing a catch – but because she was so small when we became teenagers, for instance, she was always 'the little sister'.

When she got older her personality came out more – she can be a bit like Roy; when there's crack to be had she can take over the singing duties and put on an Adele tribute act (if Adele ever reads this: you have nothing to worry about).

All the family live in Waterford, all working here.

Dad worked all his life in Waterford Crystal. At its height there were over 2,500 people working there – the biggest and by far the best employer in the town, and Dad's story, going in at fifteen and working there for over thirty years, would be a typical story for a lot of people in the town.

We were probably your typical Waterford family, come to that. Dad in the glass. Mam at home, having stopped working when she got married. Living in Hillview. Kids going to Mount Sion school, and playing hurling for Mount Sion club.

Mount Sion school is a mile from Hillview, a mile through the older part of Waterford. Walking. I probably got a lift down there when I was very young, but my memory of getting to school is by foot, along with hundreds of others.

That's something you never see now, the huge gangs of kids in their school uniforms around half past eight in the morning, all flooding through the streets. We'd all head down together from Hillview and stroll away in a group, the same as everybody else.

Nowadays I wouldn't let my own kids walk to and from school. If you're a hundred yards past a school and you see a schoolchild on their own you'd nearly think there's something suspicious going on.

For us then, walking to school wasn't even an issue: that was the only option really. Growler's mother drove, so if it was teeming down with rain we might jump in for a spin, but that was a rarity.

In 1987 there was a shadow over the school, though: there was talk that there might be a strike in the glass. We were kids in primary school and what that might mean for us didn't sink in. One lad in the class made a joke about having to hang tea bags out on the line, and that was it.

————

Looking back now, everyone working there was probably institutionalised. They paid good wages, there were so many people working there, they were working there so long – not only was the workforce institutionalised, you could say the entire town was, because everyone had depended for so long on that one factory and the wages coming out of it, directly and indirectly.

There was no shift work – it was eight to half past four – and though my father came home the odd time for lunch, when the strike eventually did come that was one of the most noticeable things: he was at home all the time. That was strange to us.

It was a huge event in the sense that we were all aware of it, and it was discussed at primary school – I was nine, Roy was eleven, the rest were even younger. It was something we knew was happening but it didn't really have that much of an impact on us. My parents were the ones who dealt with it.

As we got older we got to know other worlds, worlds beyond the street but not too distant. Across the road there was an old factory, the ACEC, which had a field next to it – a lovely square field with trees screening it from the outside, like a private field you could play in.

We had World Cups, European Championships and FA Cup finals there ... we ended up building a little shack underneath the trees which we called our dressing room. We had team meetings there before games – and these were games amongst ourselves – and discussions about tactics, all of that.

A big difference between then and now was that every

group of lads had someone with a particular skill: tree climbing. I was one of our best climbers, forty or fifty feet off the ground no problem – if I saw my own kids doing it now I'd kill them – while Billy Power was even better, an unreal tree climber.

The reason that was a vital skill? To get the ball if it was kicked up into the trees. That was the biggest disaster you could face as a nine- or-ten-year old, to see the ball lodge in the top branches – in Waterford the word was 'canted', as in 'ah lads, the ball got canted'.

And so you needed your climber. When the ACEC field got dark we'd head back to the street, where there were lights. And no trees, either. We'd sit around when we finished playing until the mothers came to the door and started calling us.

Eventually we formed a soccer team of our own. Everton and Liverpool were the big teams at the time, and the group was split on a name for our own team, before we struck a compromise: Everpool.

Padraig O'Brien (or POB) was our manager. We got black and white jerseys in Alfie Hale's sports shop, red numbers on the back. Top class. I was in goal, with a terrific black number one jersey. I was handy enough but the whole team suffered because I took the West German, Schumacher, as my role model. I was usually good for a couple of penalties to the opposition in a game.

We'd take on teams from the other streets – Marian Park, Comeragh Drive, Crescent Drive. We even had international opposition: we played the Spanish students who'd come over for the summer.

This was serious stuff: POB and Roy would go up to one or other of their bedrooms to pick the team, and we'd wait for the word. If someone wasn't picked to start, POB would say, 'We're not going with you today, we're holding you back.'

All the management-speak, but we were very serious. Ten years old, but very serious. If we won we'd spray Coca-Cola on each other like it was champagne.

The one exception I made when it came to the street soccer games was a Sunday evening, and *The Sunday Game*. I always went in to watch that.

The lads often had the right numbers out on the road, five versus five, and their game would be warming up nicely when someone would notice that Schumacher, or Ken, was missing.

I'd be on the couch watching Roscommon take on Sligo in the Connacht football championship, and they'd be raging, but I never missed it.

'Ah, we had the right numbers, where'd you go?'

'Look, *The Sunday Game* was on . . .'

There wasn't much sport on television. The hurling on screen wasn't much; the All-Ireland semi-finals and final. On a Saturday on RTE you'd have *Sports Stadium*, which could be anything – horseracing followed by badminton or hockey.

It was probably a normal childhood for a kid in the eighties. We were appreciative of what we got. I could nearly pick out on one hand the number of meals out we'd have gone for as a family, and they were probably all communions or confirmations – maybe the odd time after a match as well.

Nowadays the kids ask me where we're going for lunch on a Sunday every Sunday.

We wouldn't have gone into town that much. The middle of Waterford was only twenty minutes away by foot, but we had no interest in the journey apart from going to the cinema, the Regina on Patrick Street. At that time you'd bring in your own sweets and soft drinks – those always seemed really expensive – and settle in for the flicks.

The first one we ever went to was *BMX Bandits*, which was no award-winner, but afterwards we got on our own bikes and zoomed off to the industrial estate, copying the moves we'd just seen, no idea of the rules of the road. Innocent stuff.

Because of Dad I was noticed. We all were. When I was still in primary school one of the teachers was taking names for a skills contest and when he heard my name he asked if Pat was my dad. You'd be aware then that people were keeping an eye on you.

For us he was our hero as we grew up. He left us off, he didn't push us into playing and he didn't go to every single game and training session that we'd play. He'd go to a final, and we made plenty of finals, while nowadays I see parents at all their kids' games, and their training sessions, and I wonder if it puts pressure on them.

Dad had no problem telling you if you were good or bad in a game but he didn't pressurise us either. We were successful enough as kids: we made it to finals and we won finals, but as kids we wouldn't have been that conscious of Mount Sion's history and what that meant. We were just children, playing away, and there were plenty of defeats along the way too –

Mooncoin were in the city leagues back then and were very good at the time.

St Saviours were our main rivals in the city then rather than De La Salle or Ballygunner. The fact that Saviours came from a different part of town and you didn't know them added to that rivalry.

We played and we enjoyed it. There's no parish rule in Waterford, which many people don't realise. It's a small enough city and strict boundaries for clubs probably wouldn't work.

Someone from Tramore could play for Mount Sion and vice versa, but a lot of lads from our area would have played for Mount Sion as would a lot of players from older parts of Waterford, like Barrack Street and so on.

I was seven years old and got a goal in the De La Salle tournament under-nine semi-final, a goal that won the game and got us to the tournament final. My uncle came out onto the field and threw me up in the air: I can remember that clearly. We lost that final to St Saviours, but that encouraged me.

Not long afterwards we had a tournament in the school for the O'Grady Shield and I remember getting the winning goal in that – the whole school was watching, and I got a kick out of that.

The signs were good for me because I played a lot above my grade – I was playing U15 at eleven, for instance – which meant I was surviving against older kids. Mostly at corner-forward, in out of the way, but still.

Roy was probably our best player; he had played for Waterford in the Tony Forristal, the intercounty U14 tournament, which was something we all dreamed of doing, but I was making progress.

I knew I could play. At my own age grade I'd play centre-back, centre-field.

Jim Hennessy was the man coaching us and, like Paddy Sheridan, he left us off to play games and enjoy ourselves rather than doing drills over and over. In my memory it's always a warm summer evening and he has us playing a match amongst ourselves up in the club, which I know can't be true because there's nowhere in Ireland colder than Mount Sion's pitches.

I was holding the hurley wrong at the time, left hand on top, swapping around when I had the ball. I had to change it eventually, when my father insisted on it.

'Ah I can't change now,' I said. 'I'm too old now to change.'

Eleven years old.

'Would you stop,' he said, 'If you don't change it now it'll come against you later.'

And in two weeks' time I had it changed, and I didn't know myself. It improved me hugely.

I played on the Tony Forristal team when I was thirteen. Wing-forward. Jamie O'Meara was on that team too.

The other element was that Tony Forristal was our uncle, so there was an element of family pride involved, and it was a pretty big stage. Big crowds, a lot of attention, though not as much attention as nowadays, when a fourteen-year-old who has a good game can be discussed on social media for days and days. I was okay in the game. Nothing spectacular.

We were doing well under age with the club, though.

We won the U14 county championship that year. Celebrations were low key – back to the club for *Big Brother*, lemonade and crisps – but we began to come up against players who would become more familiar later on.

A small skilful guy from Lismore, Dave Bennett. His team-mate, a big skilful guy, Dan Shanahan. They got their revenge winning the county seven-a-side final, and the prize for that was playing before a big intercounty game. We missed out, and that was a huge disappointment.

When I was fourteen I played wing-back in the Tony Forristal tournament, and it went well for me, I had three good games. I still remember the refuelling – I was up in the house and my father was saying, 'Get that Twix into you.' No agony about nutrition then.

After the last game up in Mount Sion that weekend someone said to my father that I was the best player there, and I was delighted. When he added that he'd said the same about Paul Flynn in his time I was even happier, as Flynn had starred with Waterford in winning the All-Ireland U21 final a few weeks beforehand.

When Waterford won that U21 All-Ireland, Tony Browne was the captain. Waterford don't have so many All-Ireland titles, so he was a huge figure for us. That was a massive event at that time, we would have gone to all the U21 games; the final we went to on the train, a packed Nowlan Park, fantastic atmosphere . . . and because we won, and Tony was captain, they all came back to Mount Sion with the cup.

We were just kids, drinking Lucozade, but it was electric. A fantastic atmosphere, all of us there until four in the morning, or later, drinking the occasion in.

———

Don't forget Waterford made it to the All-Ireland minor final as well that year, and we all headed for Croke Park for that; a wet, miserable day that got worse for us when Waterford lost (after they'd won the All-Ireland semi-final. I remember we stayed on to watch the All-Ireland football semi-final which was played afterwards. Donegal and Mayo, described by some as one of the worst games ever played, but Donegal won the All-Ireland after.)

It was a huge year, and it would have given us all hope. Before that there was no light on the horizon. That might sound harsh, but it's true. Then Paul Flynn came out of nowhere and lit up the Munster minor final, which was a draw the first day; we all went to the replay, up in Cork, and it was brilliant to see them win it.

The same for the Munster U21 final, when they beat Clare in Thurles: I had a blue and white cap, the old-fashioned kind, and was one of the thousands invading the pitch in Thurles at the final whistle. It was a dream year, and the future was bright. They brought Flynn onto the U21 team for the All-Ireland final replay, and he was good, too. We knew he was good, his reputation was growing, but he exploded that season.

He needed to be good – looking at the Offaly team they beat in that All-Ireland, they had the likes of Whelehan, Rigney, Kinahan, all mainstays when they won a senior All-Ireland a couple of years later. The same with Clare in the Munster final: they had Brian Lohan, Jamesie O'Connor, Davy Fitzgerald. They came back hard in that Munster final and we had to save a penalty to keep them out, the evening getting dark, huge drama. And they went on to win two All-Irelands too.

And then the next year Kerry beat us in the senior championship. Back to square one.

But that summer, 1992, was the ultimate kids' summer for us. We were all fourteen or so, and spent the summer playing soccer on the road, playing hurling in the car park, cycling out to Tramore or Annestown, with all the crack you'd expect. One of the lads, Derek Walsh, never made it to the beach, there was always an issue with the bike; another day we brought a barbecue out to Benvoy, well pleased with ourselves until we realised we'd forgotten the matches for the barbecue. We starved for the day.

It was great: eight or ten kids bombing around the roads in Waterford, and maybe passing three or four other similar gangs on our travels. You don't see that any more. You certainly don't have kids pedalling out with a pound, or a euro, in their pocket.

For us the quandary was always the same in Tramore: take your pound and buy some chips, or chance it on the slots and maybe double your money? And after it all, a round-trip cycle of twenty miles then swimming for a few hours, you'd head up to Mount Sion to train . . . and then maybe a game of soccer on the road before going to bed. And up in the morning to do it all over again.

No wonder kids in the eighties were skinny.

When it comes to absolute stand-out events from our early teens, though, there was the time the Coke lorry turned over.

A few of us were down on the Waterford Crystal Social and Sports Club pitch-and-putt course one day when we noticed people walking through the course with Coca-Cola. Armfuls of Coke. Crates of the stuff.

We strolled up to where the road turned by the Milton Bradley factory and there it was: a Coke lorry had taken the corner too quickly and flopped over. The driver wasn't injured – he was trying to minimise the loss, saying, 'Ah lads, don't take the full crates' – and we considered how to maximise our return from the situation.

Six of us headed to Milton Bradley and got a pallet and loaded it with crates of Coke. We set a course through the industrial estate to Hillview, but we realised that the security personnel in the estate, which would have been very busy at the time, might suspect something if they saw kids lugging hundreds of cans of Coke through the place.

Brainwave. We took our tops off to cover the cans and to become more anonymous. Who'd know us without our T-shirts on? Any guilt pangs vanished when we saw a guy pull up in a car and start filling the seats with crates of Coke. Off went us skinny kids trying to lift the crates, and having to take a breather every ten yards or so.

We ended up with thirty-five cans of Coke each, and because Roy was there we took seventy home. No caffeine shortage in the McGrath house for quite a while.

On other occasions we'd head down the river to an old Coke factory. There'd be Coke left there that was just past its best-before date, and we'd walk across the bridge to get it. That was the year the movie *Stand By Me* was big, and we had it in our heads we were in the same boat, walking across a bridge and in danger from a train.

The bridge was abandoned, and we'd climb to the top, slide down the other side – desperately dangerous when you look back – and drink our Coke singing 'Stand By Me', but

---

a train flew past us one evening on a different track, and we thought we were living the movie, literally.

My father had gone from the glass since 1991 – he took the second round of redundancies because he saw the end was in sight for the glass he'd known.

His hips were in bits, though. When you're a cutter you're standing and there's water running down your side – they're prone to getting hip problems, and playing hurling for so long probably didn't help either.

He couldn't work as a result, and he wasn't the only one. You work somewhere from your mid-teens, you have a good standard of living, then it's gone. That takes huge adjust-ment, and it was hard for a lot of the lads from the glass.

But we were under a bit of pressure in the house at that time. I was thirteen, Roy was fifteen, so we were getting to an age you'd be aware of that compared to the strike in 1987. Up to then we'd have been grand without being luxurious, my father had a decent job, but it was tough for a few years after that.

We had lodgers – Spanish students, WIT (Waterford Institute of Technology) students. Because of that the four of us boys were shunted into one room, talking nonsense in bunk beds all night long; Lorna was in the box room; and my parents were in their own room.

The lodgers were downstairs in the spare room, which was then converted into a makeshift bedroom, so in the morning the mother got us all out to school, the students would go to school, then come back and get fed, then we'd get fed . . . it was full on for my mother, who was working in Fitzgerald's part-time as well.

Back then there didn't seem to be as many students in houses on their own compared to nowadays; a lot of students were in digs with families.

At first it was strange but we soon got used to the variety of people coming in through the front door, such as the Libyan guy who started saying his prayers to Mecca in front of us one time.

An Italian, Mauro, another time: I remember my mother introduced us to him and told him his plate was hot. He said yes and picked it up, burned the hands off himself. Off he went to cool his hands under the tap and then into his room; somehow he took the handle off the door.

That was Mauro's first ten minutes in the McGrath house.

We had a few hurlers stay with us over the years, and we'd puck around with them; Paul Sharkey played hurling for Louth and we'd slag him that we were well able to play with him.

That was what had to be done at the time. Nowadays kids mightn't be aware of that, but it was the eighties and early nineties and we didn't know any different, to be honest.

We'd never have gone on a sun holiday as kids but my parents were great for bringing us to different places, which is something I still do now. I'd bring my own kids to Blarney, or Wexford, or Kilkenny, or the mountains.

(That came to a head, though, when I was off the summer I got my heart operation. One morning Ali asked me where we were going; when I said I'd see, she said, 'You're not bringing me to any more gardens, if I see another castle . . .')

But that's how we were reared. Make a picnic, fill up the car and head out. We'd usually go to Benvoy, which is a beach that a lot of people even in Waterford wouldn't know.

It's unreal. A beautiful strand. When the tide is in and the sun shines you could be in Portugal: high cliffs, flat beach, safe as houses. Beautiful.

We'd go out in the summer as kids, go crazy for hours, puck the ball around . . . we'd live out there. No going back home for chips or pizza, the way we do now, though the odd time the parents would pull into Harneys of Dunhill for a drink. If they did we'd go around the back to the outdoor squash club there and puck around with the hurleys and ball until it was time to go.

They're some of the best days I can remember. All together for a day out that started at half ten or eleven o'clock and ended ten hours later; it might cost a tenner for a few sandwiches and bottles of lemonade.

I'm not a huge man for lazing around in the sun but for me that's still a brilliant day out, all the kids running around on the beach until they're knackered. I try to tell them that, and even if they don't believe me, those are the days they'll remember in thirty years' time, because I remember them from my own time. The car jam-packed and not a seat belt or a child seat being used – I can even remember trips with Lorna climbing into the front to sit on my mother's lap – and my father singing songs when he wasn't giving out about the car.

(He never had any luck with cars – over the years we moved from a couple of orange Escorts to a Cortina eventually, one with electric windows, and when I saw it had a 'new' registration, with the year instead of the old letters and numbers, I thought we were made.)

When we landed at the beach, the first question he'd ask

when we turned the corner and saw the strand would be, 'Well, how many cars are here?' And if there were none it was like hitting the jackpot in the lottery, we'd be delighted altogether, blasting the ball down off the cliff and lugging the bags down onto the beach.

When it got popular we were devastated if we saw cars there when we landed: that wasn't what we expected at all on our own personal beach.

When we got older and moved off the street, we'd use what became the ABB car park as our own personal playing area. It was forty or fifty yards wide, eighty yards long, and sealed in – the ball couldn't be canted even if you tried. We'd play full soccer games there – Barcelona would have approved of us, we were very Tiki-Taka in style, everything to feet – or we'd bring the hurleys and sliotar over and play.

Then we'd stroll down to the shop on the corner of Keane's Road with fifty pence for a twenty-nine-pence bottle of Coke and a Macaroon bar, or crisps, and sit on the wall and talk rubbish for two hours.

And that was very enjoyable until we got to about fifteen or so, and we started to feel like going out into town to talk to girls might have more to recommend it than sitting on a wall eating crisps.

My first big night out was a concert, The Stunning, in Breen's. That was the main spot at the time, very different to the scene in Waterford now, and I was fifteen and a half. It was a pretty young crowd anyway, but because it was a concert it obviously wasn't policed as tightly age-wise as a normal pub would be.

It cost seven pounds to get in and I had a tenner, so three

pounds to fund the rest of the evening. I thought I was dressed to kill and for the era I probably was: green slacks, green shirt. Snazzy. That was a time you didn't wear trainers going out, or jeans; if you did you just wouldn't get into a nightclub, so you had to dress up, to look smart.

In fairness, The Stunning put on a good show. 'Brewing Up A Storm', 'Half Past Two', all the hits, and we had a great night. It was so long ago that there was a slow set, and I danced with a girl who had a far better moustache than I could manage at that age: Tom Selleck quality.

I probably had two pints of Smithwick's. Nothing major. I wasn't into drinking in a field. That never appealed to me. Some of the lads did it, but not that much, and I never saw the point of it. Even now I'd far prefer to go out and have a drink, to be sociable, rather than sit at home drinking cans on my own.

After that we probably walked up O'Connell Street and into John Roberts Square to Supermac's for chips, or Skipper's in Patrick Street for chips, and off home. Ceilin is the same age as I was then but I wouldn't dream of letting her out like that, but times were different. Bunch of lads strolling around your home town, what could happen?

When we hit sixteen we started going out more regularly, but there were no guarantees. You might get served, you might not. There were a few spots where it was fifty-fifty, like Rourke's, and the other options were places like Peg's and The Trap, which is now Synnott's, at the far end of the town to Breen's.

It didn't help if your wingman wasn't as sophisticated, either. I went into Peg's one evening with Knoxy, one of my classmates, and we asked for two pints. The barman pulled two pints of stout and put them on the counter. Knoxy took his and started drinking it, not realising it had to be left for a minute to settle first.

A dead giveaway. The barman just pointed to the door: out.

Friday nights were the night out. There was some kind of acceptance that fifteen-year-olds were let into Breen's on a Friday night, and as you got older you graduated to Breen's on a Saturday, but that was later.

(We'd encountered drink before, of course. One time as kids we were coming back in from Benvoy and we stopped in Dunhill for ice cream, and however it happened – I'm still not sure of the details – one of the lads ended up with four cans of Guinness. Whether he paid for them or not . . . anyway, we went up to the woods and had the cans. Eight of us, four cans: half a can each, and all of us pretending to be in the horrors as we cycled home.)

That was the gang – Trigger, Growler, Moose – Jamie O'Meara, a warrior for Mount Sion for years – Hayser, Matto, as well as Der Walsh, Chick Hennessy, Pat Morrissey, Martin Walsh. We still hang around together. As a crowd we called ourselves the TFE: The Feckin' Eejits, and people would still say it the odd time if we were out together: 'Well lads, how are the TFE?'.

They all played for Mount Sion apart from Billy Power, who fell in with us when his family moved to Congress Place, but he played for De La Salle. Babs Browne, Pooch and John Cleere, who also played senior for Mount Sion, became part of the group as well later.

We go off as a group together once a year, and we've been

doing it for twenty-odd years. The distance has changed a bit – we started off heading to Ballybricken, when we were seventeen, and since we've been to Hamburg, Liverpool, Barcelona, Dusseldorf. All over. They're a great gang. They always supported me with the county, certainly, and we head out the odd time and go a bit crazy.

Not too much, though. Even feckin' eejits get sense, after all.

2

THE HURLERS OF MOUNT SION

If you don't understand what it means to be part of a GAA (Gaelic Athletic Association) club I can give a good example from my own family.

Ali doesn't play hurling. She's been to the summer camp at the club and spent the day practising her Irish dancing up in the corner of the field. No interest.

But Ali thinks she's Mount Sion, and because she thinks she's Mount Sion she is.

I'm the same. It never felt like I joined Mount Sion when I was her age, or younger. I just was Mount Sion.

When I was in Mount Sion school there were six hundred kids there. It was a big school and Br Griffey and Br Dowling pushed hurling. They were brilliant. We did a lot of hurling in the yard after school and on a Saturday morning.

In the summer you moved up to Mount Sion club. Paddy

Sheridan, who trained thousands of kids there, was our first coach. By coaching I mean leaving us to play games and enjoy ourselves, not doing drills for an hour. Just hurling. Playing the game. He's still going to matches and still supports Mount Sion; the respect everyone has for him is huge, because men like him keep GAA clubs going all over Ireland.

One of my early memories of Mount Sion has nothing to do with hurling and everything to do with the Christmas parties. They'd put on Santa Claus, sweets and soft drinks, and then a film.

When you think about it, if you offered that to kids now they'd laugh at you, but there could have been two hundred of us in the hall waiting for the film every Christmas.

From the age of nine or ten we'd head up there easily enough because there was one route where you didn't even have to cross the road to get there – the footpath from my house went around the corner, through Marian Park and in through the club gates.

And we'd spend hours there, three versus three, two versus two, hurling away – and play soccer for an hour or two maybe to break the time up, spending entire days up there. One of the lads in the club said one time when he saw us coming around the corner, 'Here's the hurling gang.' That was us.

You'd be there and the senior team would be training, so you'd puck the ball back out to them. Involved. Part of it. But we were part of it a long time before that.

Dad packed in playing for Mount Sion in 1989, when I was eleven, so I can remember him playing in the county finals of 1986 and 1988 pretty clearly.

(Eoin was the mascot in 1986: little blond head, sitting in front of the team.)

I can remember things from the games, from the preparations to going up to the club afterwards for the celebrations. Before the 1988 final against Ballygunner the school made a big push to get behind the team, banners and posters and so on, and for my father we took a bed sheet from the house for a banner. The mother wasn't too happy with the loss of a sheet, and when she saw the banner, which read 'don't be slack, give it to goal-mad Mac', her humour wasn't improved.

They drew the first game in 1988 – Dad says he was poor enough – but the second day he got off to a great start. He hit two brilliant points early on, flying it at corner-forward; he might have been thirty-six, which is old enough, but the skill was still there.

Then he got sent off, unfortunately (so was Charlie O'Sullivan, and they worked together in the glass, which probably made for an interesting Monday morning). I can remember him walking off, and Roy looked at me, and the two of us were nearly crying.

Mount Sion won the game, though, and he always maintained that his sending off was the winning of the game because it left Shane Aherne, Shiner, on his own with another player inside and they destroyed Ballygunner. 'That was the plan all along,' he'd say.

He played the following year and packed it in then. He was getting hamstring injuries and finding it hard to get over them.

It was different then. Obviously. I remember he retired from intercounty hurling in 1984 but Waterford asked him to come back two years later.

———

They were playing in Cork and he drove us up to Páirc Uí Chaoimh – my mother, Roy and himself – and he took his gear out of the boot and said, 'See ye later,' and headed into the dressing room. Nowadays he'd be gone off with the team from about nine in the morning!

In 1988 it was better again. Mount Sion made the Munster club final against Patrickswell, and the game was fixed for Thurles. There used to be a hotel outside Cashel, on a hill, and we all went up there with him to meet up with the team.

Mistake. The hotel was abandoned. We were walking around an empty building, looking in the windows, banging on doors, looking for the team. No mobiles, no way to find the other players: just us saying 'where are they?' to each other outside this creepy empty hotel, which looked like something from *The Shining*.

We ended up driving on to Thurles and making the throw-in just in time. And they lost by just a point or two. When you see how different it is now, how professional . . .

As we were getting older my father would have stressed a few things to us. One of them was pretty straightforward: don't take any shit on the field. Don't start it, but don't take it.

At times we probably took that advice too much to heart. When I was playing U14, for instance, I would have been pulling fairly wild at times – not dirty, just enthusiastic – and Peter Power, the manager, said it to me one day.

'What are you doing?'

'What do you mean?'

'You're after pulling across four or five different fellas there, Ken, you can't do that.'

He settled me down. I was probably just getting carried away and acting the maggot without really realising it, but I concentrated on hurling after that.

I had to mind myself at the same time. I was pretty young getting on teams: Paraic Duffy and the GAA probably wouldn't be too happy to hear I was playing in an East U21 county final when I was 15, for instance. We played Portlaw in that final and when the ball was thrown in I remember getting the handle of a hurley in the back; I let fly with my own hurley and that was it.

I was fifteen but I didn't care. If someone hit me I'd hit them back twice as hard. We all took that attitude in playing; you didn't have to decapitate anyone but if you didn't stand up for yourself then the word would go around fairly quick that you could be bullied, and then you *would* be bullied. The referee's attitude is that if you're on the field then you're old enough to mind yourself, and that's the right attitude.

Eoin, though . . . I remember a senior challenge game up in the club when he was just coming onto the senior team, he'd have been young enough, and this guy was giving him a hard time up in the corner.

I wasn't playing for some reason. I was standing watching the game with my father, who called out, 'Don't take that, Eoin.'

And Eoin saw red. The ball broke between him and your man and Eoin pulled hard, and all that was left of the hurley was what was in his hand. He went after his man with the six inches of broken hurley, running around in a rage, and we were saying, 'He's going to kill someone, he'll be suspended for life.' When we weren't laughing at him, that is.

I made one fair change at sixteen when I gave up my helmet. It was a beaten docket at that stage anyway – I'd had it since I was four or five – but I forgot to bring it to one game, played well in the game, an U16 county final, and decided I'd press on without it.

A minor county final, against Lismore, was probably the first time people said I had real potential. I was sixteen and got 2-7, including a goal from a free in the last minute to win the game.

The image helped – I'd gotten cut and was stitched up at the side of the field, a big bandage wound around my head like a turban, so I looked the part.

It was a good year for the club – we won the U16, minor, U21 and senior county titles, and while I was on the first three of those teams, I was asked to play senior as well. My father said no, that I was too young, and he was right. Evidence? I played minor for Waterford that same year, 1994, and I wasn't ready for it. At all.

That was a time there'd be a double-header in Fermoy, maybe a crowd of eight thousand people. The big time.

And we built it up in our heads all that year as a huge event. We had a good team – Roy, Micheal White, Dan, Bennett. The eastern lads would be collected by the bus at Norris's Corner and we'd get the western lads on board in Dungarvan.

We'd trained well, Albert Burke prepared us properly, we had a decent team, but it was too much for me. I shat myself, basically.

I told our keeper not to puck the ball out to me: I was in a heap, almost shouting down to our goal, 'Put it over that side! That side!'

We beat a good Tipperary team that night – they had Johnny Enright, Liam Cahill – and made it to the Munster final, but Cork had a terrific team. Seán Óg Ó hAilpín, John O'Flynn, they made the All-Ireland final after, and they beat us well.

We had a chance in the first half of that Munster final. David Byrne, Stunner, from Dunhill, took a shot and was convinced he hit the bar running across the inside of the goal in Thurles, that he'd scored a goal. At the time there were four or five points in it, and a goal would have made a difference, but it wasn't to be.

I came on at half-time. It was the curtain-raiser to Clare–Limerick in the senior game, so the place was full towards the end of the game. Forty thousand plus. I was nervous. I thought I was ready but I wasn't, not really. I hit a few frees and did my job, but no more than that.

Without being cocky, I knew I'd play senior for Waterford, but it was an easier time to develop. There was no focus on you on Twitter, no clips of you being put up on Facebook. You could come on at your own pace.

We were playing in the C grade of the schools competition, for instance, which is a fair distance from Broadway, but you'd come up against good players and do well against them, and that increased your confidence and your belief – without putting you in the spotlight. It all helped.

But I had no plan, really, outside of being interested in playing hurling for Waterford: that was the extent of the plan. I felt if I played for Waterford, I'd have no problem getting a good job.

I was never focused on study, or college, and I should have been. If I were seventeen again, I certainly would be. I wouldn't have done my leaving certificate while working in the glass, for instance, but I'll get back to that.

I wasn't a messer in school. I didn't misbehave, I just wasn't motivated to study. I'd do an hour's study and nearly collapse, while Roy would do four or five hours' study, no problem. I'd cram in some work the evening before a test and that'd be it.

As an example of my level of interest, we'd have been playing a lot of games for the school. You'd be told on Wednesday that there was a game Friday, bus leaving the school at eleven o'clock.

I'd deliberately leave my gear at home and rock up to school on Friday: 'Oh no, I thought the game was Monday.' I'd then walk home and get my gear, missing a couple of hours' worth of lessons in the process. I wanted to do well in the tests, I just wasn't interested in doing enough of the work to do well in the tests.

I got a job in the glass my last two summers in school: first in the maintenance department, as a fitter's mate – getting tools and equipment for them – and then as a carpenter's mate, doing a similar job.

One of those summers, 1995, was unbelievable, a real heatwave, and because the roof was being tarmacadamed, I spent most of the summer going off for ice cream and water for the lads who were doing the work.

I was seventeen, playing on the Waterford minor team, and the lads were telling me, 'Get into the shade out of

34

the sun, you've a match tomorrow, drink plenty of water.'

I clocked in. Clocked out. Loved it. There would have been a job there for me in the stores, or an apprenticeship, and I was half-tempted to stay there, but I'd applied to do production engineering in college, and I said I'd give it a go.

I wasn't academically driven enough to do well in college, though. I got a scholarship to do sport and recreation in Waterford IT, so I transferred to that. I never really took to it.

Intercounty games were part of that, particularly championship games in the summer. Because there was no back door, straight knockout, it became an even bigger event for us, and we had our routine.

We'd go to Cashel and stop there to have sandwiches out of the boot of the car, and there'd be half a dozen more cars there, people doing the same. We got to know them and they us over the years, which is hardly surprising given how small the numbers were going to Waterford games – you might have five or six thousand people at a game, half of them from the other county.

After the sandwiches, back into the car and off to the game itself, which was almost always in Thurles, and which helped my crowd obsession.

Ever since I was a small child I've been fascinated with crowds and stadiums, and when we'd go into Semple Stadium, as kids, I'd be saying to Roy, 'Look over at the New Stand, there's definitely four sections full there.' He'd tell me to knock it off, of course, he'd want to watch the game.

As a kid I'd be drawing sports stadia in my school books, on my copies. Weird stands and terraces, scoreboards, the heads of the spectators . . . Roy played a match up in

Kilmacthomas once as a kid and I interrogated him about the ground – 'What's the bank like?' 'It's steep, yeah.' Quizzing him about Kilmac like he'd just played in the Nou Camp.

When I got to play in some of them as a kid I was worse. We played an U14 game up in the Gaelic Grounds in Limerick and I was delighted, running around exploring the stand, running up to the back of the terrace to look down the other side – and I dropped my hurley.

Disaster. I could see it lying on the ground down below, fifty feet away, but that side of the ground was locked up, and I couldn't find a groundsman to let me in to get it. I had to play with someone else's hurley and had a stinker of a game, and that taught me a lesson: I'd have to calm down a bit about the obsession with stadiums.

Maybe it's something to do with Walsh Park, which wasn't an impressive ground when I was a kid, and I wanted to see Waterford play in big games, in a big stadium.

That was rare enough. We went to the league semi-final in 1987 in Croke Park, when Waterford got hammered, but disappointed as we were, at least we'd been to Croke Park. In 1989 Waterford made the Munster final in Páirc Uí Chaoimh and were well beaten by Tipp, who were at their peak (I can guarantee yours truly was at the game saying, 'There's more on the Tipp terrace than there is on ours.')

I'm a lot better now but I'd still be interested in crowds and attendances. Even now. If we go into a ground to watch a game I'll be saying, 'There's definitely seven thousand here, definitely,' and the rest of them will be laughing at me. We were in New York once and I enjoyed going to Madison Square Garden, the same with Barcelona when I was over there with a few lads on a stag – I enjoy having a look around, what's wrong with that?

Only last year we were all at a match somewhere and Roy was sitting next to me.

'Fair crowd here today,' he said.

'Yeah, there's probably a few thousand there, and over there another couple of thousand.'

Sure he was only winding me up, they were all sitting behind me laughing their heads off at me.

In 1996 I was in the college, playing away. We won the Freshers All-Ireland, beating a good UCC (University College Cork) team which featured Joe Deane and Johnny Enright up in Ballyduff. We had Colm Cassidy from Offaly and a few more, and it was a good win; we were eleven points down at half-time but came back to win it. We piled into Preacher's that night celebrating. It was an All-Ireland, after all.

My heart wasn't in it, though. The year before, the summer of 1995, I'd been getting three hundred pounds a week in my summer job in the glass – very good money, particularly for a seventeen-year-old.

I was immature, basically. There were continuous assessments on the course, and I didn't turn up for some of them; a lot of the lads were cute enough to get most of their marks in the bag long before the summer exams even started. I failed a few of those summer exams, though, and I just never went back to repeat them. With the scholarship I had to do summer coaching – they weren't formal summer camps so much as street leagues – and I started in Teva/Norton, the pharmaceutical factory, at the end of August 1996.

It was a decent job and I settled, worked there for five years, and when I left I was twenty-three. At that time I thought I was too old to go back to college, which is ridiculous, but I was probably too focused on hurling. I should have picked something and focused on it in terms of a course, but I didn't.

3

Defeats and Diets: The Gerald Years

I went to the 1995 All-Ireland final fresh from my debs dance. True story.

We had the debs on the Thursday beforehand, we played the U21 championship on the Friday and the manager let us out afterwards.

Then, Saturday morning, road trip: about ten of us piled into the back of a van and hit north for the All-Ireland Sevens in Kilmacud. We crashed in Jury's Christchurch and played in the sevens – we had Pat Ryan, Padraig Fanning, my brother Roy, and they sneaked me into a few pubs, past the bouncers looking down at this blond kid holding his breath. Great night.

The following morning Pat Ryan found a ticket for me and we were up on the terrace, screaming for Clare as though it were Waterford. We were delighted they'd won, they were like heroes to us because they'd made that breakthrough, seeing the likes of Seánie McMahon and Anthony Daly win an All-Ireland . . .

Everyone loves an underdog – I'm sure that's why people supported Waterford many times over the years – and Clare had more than that going for them. The likes of Daly, Jamesie O'Connor, the Lohans, they were a team with characters. Personalities. That coincided with the big Guinness sponsorship deal, the glamour of all of that.

And because we were on the periphery, we wanted in. The 1995 Munster senior championship ended badly for Waterford, a big fight against Tipperary in Cork, so we were a bit off the top, but we had hopes. Bright signs.

And a good example not too far away. We'd been to three Munster minor finals, and if we'd lost them we'd competed, at least; Clare themselves had gone down in two Munster senior finals before winning one.

I played minor for Waterford in 1995 and we won the U21 county final with the club. I'd scored four points in the senior county final off Fergal Hartley, but Ballygunner beat us in a replay. Huge crowd in Walsh Park. There was a lot of focus on me because I got the four points off the stick. I didn't handle the ball for any of them – one I volleyed over and the others I flicked up and hit over the bar to score.

That was the big arrival for me, that county final. My father was good, he wouldn't have interfered or given me detailed instructions – he told me to enjoy the occasion and to play away. It was a big game; Ballygunner had won the county in 1992, we'd won it in 1994, but their good team was coming.

We threw that game away. We were five points up coming towards the end – I remember thinking, 'my first county final and I'm going to win a medal' – but they got a couple of goals and beat us. I was just seventeen, I'd played well enough: progress.

When we won the county U21 title we went out and celebrated, naturally, and the next day Roy and I were asked to come along to a national hurling league game. It was a pre-Christmas game, not exactly high profile. Tipperary were the opposition and they didn't have their big guns out before Christmas, and I was happy enough sitting on the bench.

I came on in one of the next games, though, against Galway. Fergal Hartley picked up an injury in the first minute and I was thrown on. Marking Gerry McInerney.

Gerry McInerney! White boots. All-Ireland medals. Long hair. I don't think I took the ball in my hand once – I pulled on absolutely everything, let fly without once putting my hand to the ball. I got a point and everyone said I'd done well (which will tell you how much the game has changed – nowadays if you were pulling on everything you'd be destroyed by management for just hitting the ball away and not holding onto possession).

It was intimidating on one level: he was well known, I was still only seventeen, there was a big crowd in Dungarvan for the game, but I enjoyed it. We only lost by a point and Galway were going well that time.

That defeat put us out of contention for the league play-offs, so there was a fairly low-key build-up to the next game. I was on the bus after a winning a game with the college when my name was announced on the radio: starting against Offaly.

Offaly: Brian Whelehan of the Millennium team, one of the greatest hurlers of all time. I'd say, though, if you were to ask him about that game it mightn't be one of his career highlights. It was a nothing league game and he was marking a young fella he'd never heard of, but I enjoyed the experience. It wasn't a great day, I got a point or two but Whelehan . . . he just did whatever he wanted, basically. He was that good: he'd play his own game so I was thinking, 'Sure there's no point in trying to mark him.' He was at his ease.

People know I played senior championship for Waterford when I was a minor back in 1996 thanks to TG4's *Laochra Gael*, which showed me in all my T-shirted glory getting inter- viewed by Marty Morrissey after that game. Tony Mansfield was the manager and Gerry Fitzpatrick, who came in with us when Justin McCarthy took over, was the physical trainer.

We trained hard for that game, but looking back now, you wouldn't say it was that scientific compared to the way teams train nowadays. You were flogged in training, doing laps and laps, because Clare had introduced savage physical training and every team was trying to match it.

I didn't mind the training – I was eighteen and fit enough, and because I was on the minor and U21 teams I was going back and forth between the teams. Mostly I trained with the seniors, because they were playing Tipperary at home in Walsh Park: everything was focused on June 2nd, that date, because it was straight knock-out. If you lost that evening then your summer was over if you were a senior hurler.

I was nervous that morning, certainly. I remember going for a stroll and the game being on my mind. One of the older lads had said to me a couple of weeks beforehand, 'You're going to be surprised by the speed of this game when it starts, championship hurling is crazy fast,' and I think I took that too much to heart. When I played I didn't find it as fast as he'd said, though I'd probably built it up myself in the lead-up to a situation where I was expecting the speed to be nearly superhuman.

I survived. I was marking Raymie Ryan and I got a point, and I was so delighted I slapped the hurley off the ground, but after that I caught a good ball and gave away a free for overcarrying – I probably did take too many steps, in fairness – and they landed the free downfield and got a goal, which was the turning point.

In the second half I was only okay. People were encouraging but I didn't think I'd been that good. I felt I contributed something without starring. It was an anticlimax at the end, to be out of the championship.

That interview I gave Marty I don't remember at all: it only came back to me when I saw it on *Laochra Gael* and I had my head in my hands looking at it. Eighteen years old and doing an interview on the television after a game – another difference between then and now. There's no manager would send a teenager out like that to talk, and if he did he'd have plenty of media training first!

That's how it was back then; players weren't hidden away as much. That never bothered me either way. I was happy enough to chat. I always read the papers before and after games, though a lot of players say they don't.

That said, I wouldn't go out of my way to get a paper the Sunday of a game, for instance, but if there was a copy around I wouldn't avoid it either. I always felt it was just someone's opinion of a game or a player, so it didn't seem that big a deal to me.

As things got more professional at intercounty level you ended up going places and hanging around for longer before games or training: you were killing time in a hotel for a couple of hours, so if someone pulled out a paper you'd read it.

Looking at the interview with Marty now you'd swear I hadn't a care in the world, but at that age you'd be thinking, 'I've this to look forward to for years.' We went out for dinner, the team, and then I hooked up with my own crowd in Preacher's.

Our main men were Damien Byrne, Stephen Frampton, Fergal Hartley, Tony Browne, Sean Daly, Billy O'Sullivan, Jimmy Beresford, Paul Flynn – we had a decent enough team. Tipp beat us by a goal and lost the Munster final afterwards in a replay, so you'd have said we weren't too far away.

I was playing mostly as a forward then. Centre-forward playing minor for Mount Sion, getting 2-7 in that county final, forward with the county minors and taking the frees, wing-forward with the club senior team, but I'd always played centre-back at my own age, and I always liked it. Any chance I had to go back to centre-back I took it, and I was playing there the odd time for the club U21s and I had some of my best games that year there.

Not that I turned down invitations to play up front when they came. I was invited to play for the Rest of Ireland against Wexford the week after they won the All-Ireland in 1996, the traditional Wednesday-night game for charity.

I played a minor game the day before that game and the lads were slagging me, going off to play for the Rest of Ireland along with Tony Browne. Wexford Park was mobbed, a real carnival atmosphere, and I ended up marking Larry O'Gorman. At that stage Larry was after three days of celebrating an All-Ireland, and his focus was elsewhere, to put it mildly. I got the ball at one stage and flicked it over his head and then pointed it: a great score, and I was delighted with myself.

Larry came past me, going out the field: 'Don't do that again, Ken.'

'Okay, okay.'

And I didn't.

We got a Rest of Ireland jersey each, which was a great souvenir to pack into your gearbag, and we stayed on for a great night with the Wexford lads. And that was a boost, getting to line out with these guys from other counties and holding your own. Getting used to the atmosphere.

It was a quick rise but I took it in my stride, really. The progress wasn't scrutinised: you played on Sunday and the *News and Star*, the local paper, would have the report on the Wednesday. Nowadays a player does well in an U16 game and there are a thousand tweets about it, or a clip from someone's phone of a goal he scored is on Facebook, and people saying it's the goal of the year.

That's pressure. Our time was far more innocent. We'd go to U21 training with the county together – myself, Roy, Derek McGrath, Moose, Trigger and a couple more – and we'd have ice cream on the way back. Chatting. Music on the car radio. No stress.

At the end of 1996 Gerald McCarthy came in. There was a meeting and we were told he was going to take over as manager, simple as that, and that things were going to change.

I wouldn't have seen him playing, he played in his last All-Ireland final the year I was born, but I was excited by the prospect. Getting a high-profile manager like that in promised to be an advance. Professionalism. Progress.

I missed out on the pre-season training they were doing out in Dunhill early in 1997, but the reports coming back were unanimous. It was tough going.

Looking back now, Gerald was obviously trying to find out who'd be with him for the next few years – who were the players who could take the punishment in training, who could stand up to it.

My first real encounters with him bore that out. Coming into 1997 I was beginning to fill out, to grow into a man, really. I was still eighteen, nineteen but I was getting bigger and – I thought – stronger, but Gerald disagreed. When I met him he told me I'd have to lose weight. To go on a diet.

I remember saying I loved my food, and I went out in the next game and scored a few points, thinking, 'A diet, I don't need a diet.' I was skinny enough growing up – Chubby Checker and the Fat Boys had a big hit one summer when I was a teenager, for instance, and the rest of the lads disqualified me from singing the song because they said I wasn't fat enough.

But Gerald was right. My body was adjusting to growing up, basically, and I needed to keep an eye on what I was putting into it. There's photographic evidence to back up Gerald's position, too – a picture of me on the wall in Mount Sion getting young hurler of the year for the second time. It isn't too flattering, and not because of my fashion choices.

It was a frustrating year, because Gerald was getting to know us and we were getting to know his ways. He was a very approachable, very friendly guy, but he also carried an aura, a Cork attitude, something that came from winning so many All-Irelands, achieving everything you could achieve in the game. A swagger.

We'd go into Thurles, or Limerick, or Páirc Uí Chaoimh, and everyone was over to talk to him, to say hello. A challenge game anywhere in the country, there'd be people who'd know him and were mad to chat to him, to be in his company.

And so were we. Delighted to be strolling in after him, delighted to be part of the entourage.

He was professional, though. Strict. He dropped Dan, Ray Barry, Sean Daly. Lads who'd been with Waterford for years. He put an end to the drinking culture.

It was frustrating, though. Limerick beat us by a few points in the championship that year, and we were gone. All over for an entire twelve months.

Apart from the league, which the GAA had decided would run through the summer. We ended up playing Antrim a week *after* (we lost to Limerick in the championship: lost to Limerick on a Sunday, on a downer for a few days, trained the Thursday after, and out again in Walsh Park the following Sunday in the league).

We won, and afterwards we all went out to Jack Meade's for a few drinks. It was a beautiful summer's day, scorching sun, and I remember distinctly looking forward to the following season. I was thinking that things were only starting.

In 1997 I played for Munster in the Railway Cup. Myself and Tony were the only Waterford lads on it so we headed up together, but we mixed away with the other players, no bother. In the first game on a Saturday evening – it was all run off over a weekend – we played Connacht, or Galway, and I was going well up in the forwards, seeing plenty of the ball.

I flicked the sliotar down to myself at one stage and Nigel O'Shaughnessy from Galway tried to flick it away from me; he missed the ball and connected with my mouth: bang. All my teeth were blown out, scattered around the field.

It wasn't that sore, looking back. I was more annoyed than anything else. I played on and then headed off to the hospital in Ballinasloe, but they couldn't do anything for me: I'd have to see a dentist, and that could only happen the following Monday.

When I got back to the hotel Michael Ryan and Conal Bonnar from Tipperary, and Tony, were there. A lot of the north Tipp and Clare lads had tipped away home, so the four of us were the only ones staying over.

Someone eventually said, 'Will we go for a pint?'

I was thinking, 'Sure I won't be playing tomorrow, I'll relax and have a couple.' I hadn't a tooth in my head so I ended up drinking beer through a straw. We hit every pub in Ballinasloe and then piled back to the hotel. A wedding. Great.

We crashed the wedding reception and the night carried on. Tony was running around the wedding party with a sheet over his head, pretending to be a ghost – he loves that kind of thing. It all continued into the small hours and we had a great chat with Michael and Conal, who were coming towards the end of their own time playing, and they were talking about the potential Waterford had, that we weren't far away. And we agreed, of course.

———

The following morning I got a phone call: how was I fixed?

'Grand,' I said. 'I'll play.'

I got a couple of points and we won, beat Leinster, and on the way home I remember saying to Tony, 'This is brilliant.' There weren't great crowds at the Railway Cup games then but it was a bit more prestigious than it is now. There was more attention paid to it and lads took it more seriously, even if they could end up running around a wedding the night before the final dressed up like a ghost. I was delighted on the road home to Waterford to have picked up a medal.

I was delighted until I got to the dentist the Monday morning, anyway. I wouldn't be a great fan of the view from the dentist's chair at the best of times, and having the remains of my front teeth whipped out that day didn't change my mind, but I was still happy with the weekend. And that gave me confidence with Waterford in turn – that I was able to hold my own in that company.

I've always said that a mixture of Gerald and Justin would be the perfect manager. Gerald was always able to get a team up for a game, he knew just how to do that. In 1998 and 1999 we played some brilliant hurling, but I also felt that we let him down, to be honest. He couldn't have done any more in those years – he looked after players on and off the field, anything he could sort out for us, he'd do.

Shane Aherne did the physical training that time, and he didn't spare us. The back of the stand in Dungarvan saw fair suffering. Again, we were all trying to top what Clare were doing at the time, or what they were supposed to be doing, and it got crazy. One night in Dungarvan we were put through eighty sprints. Eighty.

And we did them. Fifteen laps to start off, and Seán Culli-nane would take off, leading at full speed, and set a savage pace. Gerald stationed men on each cone, and if you cut inside the cone you got extra laps.

When I say it was old-school training, I'm not joking. We were doing circuit training in the back of the stand in Dungarvan. If you're wondering where the gym was, don't bother. We did the circuit training in the toilets. Literally. Chin-ups in the toilet cubicles, all of that. It was like *Rocky IV* and we were out in the wilderness.

I never saw fellas as fit. Nobody could hide. If you did, you were gone. Two hours, two and a half hours. These days there's so much science involved that it'd probably be dismissed as madness, but we had to do it. We had to get up to the levels being set by the likes of Clare and Limerick and Wexford, who were good hurlers but were also powerful, strong men.

Clare in particular. I remember a Railway Cup game being on in Ennis the same time that Clare were getting their All-Ireland medals, a massive function in the West County. You could see the crowds of people milling around, trying to get photographs taken with the players – no selfies with the mobiles they had at that time – and we wanted something similar, no doubt about it. That had an impact, because we were on the periphery of it.

Hurling was taking off in that period of the nineties: Guinness was sponsoring the games and marketing them very well; huge crowds, huge interest, and we felt we could compete. Hartley, Tony, Brian Greene – we had good players driving it on, fellas who wanted to succeed, and Gerald's arrival coincided with that.

And his approach worked. Dungarvan old-school training had its effect. Seán Cullinane had an unbelievable six-pack when nobody had a six-pack. Everyone was flying.

Then, on top of that, you had the famous NuTron Diet.

We were back in October 1997 training for the following year, and it was very tough. I'd never trained that hard: really we were getting the training done that you'd normally expect to do in January or February, so we were miles ahead when we came to 1998, but it was a tough slog that autumn.

Then Gerald announced we'd be on a new diet on January 6th. The NuTron Diet. I think the Offaly footballers had been on it in the summer of 1997, and they'd won the Leinster championship, so it was in vogue.

There was a system to it. You went to a clinic for a blood test, your sample was sent off to a lab where they determined the best foods for you and the foods which didn't suit you. All the lists were individualised, so come January we all trooped into the clinic in town for our blood tests.

Myself, Derek McGrath and Roy, my brother, had a last blow-out in The Old Stand on the Saturday before the diet kicked in. We knew it was the last chance of a few drinks before we got our lists of what was allowed and what wasn't, and we took it.

Come the Monday we got the lists, we were warned not to eat food on our 'forbidden' list, because if we did we'd put on a load of weight. Off we went.

People bought into it. The whole team – and Gerald and the back-room lads – followed their lists, and when word seeped out to the public they bought into it. If you were out having a coffee someone would say to you, 'Hey, is that on your list? I'm watching that.'

On my diet I'd have to have rashers for my breakfast; I couldn't have bread or milk but I could eat rice. Other lads had different foods they couldn't have, though alcohol was an absence on everyone's list. Every Friday you went down to the clinic to be weighed, and lads were nervous: 'What did you lose, what did you gain?' There were fantastic rumours – if you sneaked a Mars Bar you'd put on five pounds, supposedly. Fellas got paranoid altogether about their weight.

But it was fantastic to bring the whole team together. Everyone was in it as a group, and supporting each other and encouraging each other. I was out in Norton's having a full stir-fry at half eleven in the morning, and even though I wasn't a great man for vegetables I'd cram them in.

I was fit enough before we started, but I was flying come January and February when we played the South East League, which was then the pre-season tournament, and we won it. We beat Cork down in Walsh Park in the final. A trophy. A title.

It rolled on from there. We won our first league game, against Tipperary up in Thurles and we hit over twenty points. I was on John Carroll, who I'd marked at minor level, and I wanted to see if I'd improved. I hit six or seven points from play and felt I'd come on. I don't know how seriously he was going at that time of the year, but I felt I'd progressed after that game. Even a Tipp man – Francie Thompson – in Mount Sion said it to me.

We were allowed out after that game and lads were

destroyed, of course. No drink for weeks, we were gone after a couple of pints. On the floor. We ended up laughing at each other in Club LA, we were so happy.

Because we won the South East League we got a weekend away as a prize. In Dublin, nowhere exotic, though we were out in Kilternan, near the ski slope. First team in Ireland to go cold-weather training, maybe.

On the Friday evening Gerald was saying we weren't to go out for a drink, but you get to know a manager, and you get to know the difference between a serious 'lads, no drinking' and a not-so-serious 'lads, no drinking'.

This fell into the latter category, and it ended up as a session. I wouldn't like to give the impression that it was all boozing whenever we could, but we'd been training for six months solid at that stage. We had plenty of hard work done. Provided you don't go overboard, a blowout like that can bond a team and bring fellas out of themselves.

And that's what happened that weekend. We were in a hotel, there was a nightclub in the hotel, and soon enough we were out on the dance floor. To give some impression of staying on the straight and narrow most of the lads were drinking Bacardi Breezers, which almost suggested we were drinking orange and lemonade. Almost.

We trained the following morning and because the Grand National was on in the afternoon, we were left to our own devices. Lads were going here, there and everywhere but about ten of us found a nice spot, a pub called The Silver Tassie, on the old road into Dublin. We had one of the best days we ever had, just slagging each other, enjoying the horseracing. Great crack.

Back to the hotel, into Bray on a bus for dinner and a couple of drinks. Brilliant. I remember clearly thinking, 'Yeah, this is what it's all about; this is a team.'

That was important because, as ever, there were plenty of rumours and whispers around that time, that certain clubs didn't get on with other clubs, that fellas didn't want to play together. It was nonsense. Mount Sion lads were getting lifts to training off Ballygunner lads for years, no problems at all, but people can't help themselves, putting rumours around.

It was the first time, though, that we'd had that experience as an intercounty team. All together, all having the crack, but all focused on what we were going to do on the field as well.

I still laugh any time I pass that pub. We had great crack that day – that weekend – and it was the start of it, really. The great years.

The club is part of you because it's always been part of you. It's not a choice. It's just part of growing up. We weren't interested in another sport, really. There was soccer, and you'd be interested, but it was all about Mount Sion, really. You heard about the players in the past – Frankie Walsh and Larry Guinan, all of them, and the likes of my own father and Jim Greene, and Pat O'Grady and Pat Ryan, all of them down the years.

You're in the school and the club wins a county title – the next day they're down in the schoolyard with the cup, the captain telling you there's a half-day and no homework, one of the best days in the year.

It was a natural thing. You'd go up and play away for hours. I often went up there for hours on my own – the seniors would be training and because there wasn't a great net behind the goals, if the ball went over the fence I'd be off hunting around the car park for it and I'd drive it back out to them.

We played Gaelic football for a while, too. I remember winning U14 A hurling and football, and we ended up going to the two Féile tournaments, for instance.

For the hurling Féile, the All-Ireland side of it, we went to Galway. We had a good team – unbeaten for a few years in all competitions in Waterford – and we fancied ourselves.

We were playing Loughrea in the first game and, back then, with no Twitter or Facebook, we had no idea if they were good, bad or indifferent. Off we went on the bus, landed into Galway, got a great feed off the host families – and Loughrea beat us out the gate. Hammered us. Half of us couldn't move with the mashed potatoes and roast beef inside us.

We won another couple of games, against an Offaly team and a Galway team, but we didn't qualify out of the group stage. An eye-opener. Me and John O'Keeffe stayed that weekend with a family called Kennedy – their son Gregory played hurling for Galway later – and we had another eye-opener when we drove their tractor around the fields: we nearly went down a dyke with it, an adventure O'Keeffe still reminds me of.

The football Féile was held up in Meath. We would have been decent but . . . traditional in our approach to football. Old-fashioned. Fellas were athletic and competitive, but when we got older we were too busy with the hurling to pay too much attention to football. Still, we played Munster club championship against a Kerry team one year.

It was a quirk in the Waterford club structures that got us into that competition. We got to the 2006 junior county semi-final, and lost, but because we were the last remaining team in that competition that was unattached – that didn't have a senior team – we were the only team eligible to play in the junior club championship. We ended up taking on Duagh from Kerry.

We'd won the county hurling title that year, so anything after that was a bonus. This was an adventure, pure and simple. We were at home so a temporary stand was put up – luckily enough, because Duagh came to Waterford in busloads. Hundreds of them.

I overheard a couple of them talking beforehand, saying Mount Sion wouldn't be bad if they had so many intercounty hurlers. If they thought there was going to be an ambush, though, they weren't long relaxing.

One of the first balls fired out to the middle landed between me and this youngster from Duagh, and he took off into the air, caught it with one hand and had my head caught in his other hand, holding me off to one side.

I said to myself, 'This is going to be a long afternoon.' I'd never seen a man get up so high in the air. I recognised him later with the Kerry senior team: Anthony Maher.

We did manage a goal at one stage – Micheal White finished off the move and celebrated by doing a Klinsmann dive into the corner of the field – but they were well on top. I was taking a sideline kick over in front of their supporters and I heard one of the young lads saying, 'Ah, wait 'til you see the state of this.'

Jinxed. I ballooned it straight back out over the sideline.

They should have realised how seriously we were taking

it from our warm-up – they were doing drills to get their touch in over in one half of the field, while we were crossing the ball in soccer-style down in our half. They were good company afterwards, though; they stayed on and we had a great night in the club.

I was never in a ball alley in my life. Back then Mount Sion didn't have one – there's a great ball alley there now, and an AstroTurf pitch, but when I was starting, there was the main pitch and the school pitch, where we did most of our training.

It was all hitting around in twos. We had a game in the car park where one would go into each goal, about fifty to sixty yards away, and we'd try to score goals against each other. It was good for your first touch – and your accuracy, because you had to keep it low in order to score a goal. You were driving the ball at each other, stopping them, returning them – practising the skills all the time, just not in a drill environment.

With frees, I was never obsessed with them. I had a funny attitude – to me it was all about scoring from play and contributing from play rather than from frees. If I got twelve points from frees I'd nearly be disappointed, and if I missed ten frees I wouldn't be bothered because I always felt I could contribute something from play instead.

When I got to my twenties I'd have spent hours on my own training but doing physical work rather than hurling. And when I say physical, I mean running rather than gym work. The gym only came in for us during the mid-noughties.

The skill and the touch came fairly naturally, without being big-headed about it, particularly after my father took a couple

---

of weeks to change my grip to the correct one. There were things I wouldn't have practised too much because, to be honest, I didn't see the point of them.

Sideline cuts, for instance – I'd see lads practising them for ages and it wouldn't make sense to me to give so much time to that. I would have thought I had more to my game than that; I'd often go up to the club for hours, for instance, taking shots from different parts of the field to get my eye in.

Fielding the ball was never an issue, I did it pretty naturally, but when helmets became compulsory it affected my fielding. I nearly became more jibbery – a Waterford term for nervous – because of the helmet, or maybe it was the injuries all kicking in, but compared to the time I fielded the ball in my prime, it was certainly different.

Growing up there were players I admired, of course. Ciarán Carey was a different player to me; he ran with the ball more than I did, but I loved his attitude, his ability to take it on. John Fenton, Tony O'Sullivan, Nicky English – their skill was unbelievable. A guy like Tony Keady then, his attitude was inspirational. Going up the field in an All-Ireland final and putting the ball over the bar. Peter Finnerty the same, and later the likes of Larry O'Gorman and Martin Storey.

You can probably pick out the era I grew up in because there aren't that many Kilkenny players there; Cork and Galway were probably the two top teams when I started to notice the intercounty scene. We had our own stars in Waterford – Stephen Frampton, Hartley, Tony was our hero growing up in particular.

Clare had been heroes to us. That's not an exaggeration. They'd been to Croke Park in September and they'd brought it home.

But a day came when they weren't distant any more. Early in 1998 I went up to mark Seánie McMahon in a tournament game up in north Tipperary, and I got ten points. Man of the match award; a cheque for one hundred pounds from the organisers.

Grand, I was thinking.

The only issue was that Seánie had put down a winter celebrating a second All-Ireland title, and I was a teenager at the peak of his fitness.

I learned those lessons myself later on. You'd get the hang of tapering your training, to peak later in the year when you needed to rather than February. Nowadays it's different, the players are as fit as they'll get by the end of January and they maintain it, but back then you'd see lads carrying a bit of timber in the spring, then working unbelievably hard to come right for the summer.

I wasn't quite twenty, Seánie had had a good Christmas – he didn't have Brian Lohan behind him either that night in north Tipperary, which made the whole experience a little easier for me. Come the summer, Seánie McMahon would be a different prospect.

We were moving well that year. Fit, determined, confident – I picked up a couple of man of the match awards before we played the league semi-final in Thurles. Limerick in a double-header, Cork playing Clare the same day – and forty thousand at it, too.

Gerald threw me in full-forward against Limerick, which was something he'd do the odd time. After ten minutes Billy O'Sullivan gave me a brilliant pass for a goal, which wasn't something I was known for (in all my time I only ever got one goal in the championship, against Westmeath in a qualifier game; I hit a free from about a hundred yards and it squirted in over the line, and I was shouting up, 'who scored, did I score, is that mine?', and all of them laughing at me trying to claim the goal.)

We were good against Limerick, the whole team was so fit it was unbelievable. Seán Cullinane, Fra, all the experienced lads were in savage condition and we were in charge that day.

Ciarán Carey came on for Limerick that same day, and there was a massive cheer. It was strange for me, seeing my favourite player come on to the field for the team I was up against. I'd always admired his attitude – no-nonsense, get on with it – and Limerick had been down when he'd come on the scene, helping them get back to the top.

Still, I remember thinking, 'I'm not letting him dominate here'. I blocked him at one point and robbed the ball to get a point. It was a good score, a vital score, and I was thinking, 'We're different this year'. Micheal White got a brilliant goal to seal it late on; he flicked the ball over a defender and finished it into the corner.

We stayed on to watch the first half of Clare versus Cork, and Cork were on top when we were leaving. It was clear that Clare weren't going full out for the win, and the rumours weren't long going around that they'd trained like dogs the morning of the game, but we weren't bothered. We were in a national final, and with the permission of managers we headed out for a few pints. Bank holiday Sunday, we were out, we were in the limelight and we were enjoying it.

We had it easy enough, though. Nobody was taking a picture on their smartphone if you were having a couple of beers, but you could tell the profile of the team was building. We were young – I was twenty, Dan a year older, Bennett twenty, Micheal White twenty-one – and the style of hurling we played was attractive. We'd been down a long time, too, so the public was sympathetic to us, and there were always a few characters who could express themselves: we weren't seen as robots, certainly. People responded to us.

The league final was a reasonable copy of a championship game – a scorching hot day, a big crowd in Thurles, and two teams all out for the win. Cork had been out of the limelight a couple of years themselves, and we were desperate for silverware.

I was centre-forward on Brian Corcoran and got a score early on – slipped the corner-back and put it over, and coming outfield after hitting it the atmosphere struck me. It was electric, as it often was back then – not because I'm giving it the old 'it was better in my day' but the game was different. The centre-back would hit it long and the crowd would respond, and the opposing centre-back would return it – more noise. That doesn't happen as often in the modern game.

Corcoran got on top as the game wore on. I'd started well but by the second half he was dominating the game, not just me. He showed his experience – 'you've a bit to go yet' – without saying it out loud. That wouldn't have been his way. Good to read the game, very strong, and even though people might question his pace, he was never caught. Always in the right place, ahead of the play.

Learning my trade against the likes of him was a huge benefit to me. He was man of the match in that game but what I learned that day was as good to me as hitting seven or eight points. I also got a wicked blow in the eye when I went in to block down Fergal Ryan at one point, and it probably set me back a bit, but no excuses: I was out-hurled.

It was one of the first times at senior level we came up against players we'd face for the next decade. Seán Óg, Joe Deane, all those lads. We knew them as minors, and as seniors they showed that eighties-type Cork arrogance: 'We're Cork, this is Waterford, we'll beat them'.

Diarmuid O'Sullivan was another, though we had a little history. We'd marked each other at minor level in Fermoy: he was centre-back for Cork and I was marking him, and we'd broken hurleys off each other. Didn't give an inch. In that minor game I remember thinking, 'This guy isn't stopping, he's tough,' and years after that we were on an All-Star trip and he told me he'd been thinking the same thing. When I went off that evening I hadn't a knuckle safe, and he was the same.

We fought to the end and were disappointed to lose, but we felt it was the start, not the end. We had our eyes on the championship, after all. We were in the mix. We'd done all that savage training and we could see the benefit of it. Unscientific it might have been, but we were strong and fit and knew we'd last the course.

A few weeks after the league final, of course, we were nearly dumped out of the championship. We only scraped past Kerry in our first game. With a few minutes to go it was a draw, down in Tralee, and every one of us knew well that it had only been five years since Kerry had beaten us – in Walsh Park, at that. Some of the lads had been on the field that evening, and the memories were bubbling up.

———

Dan hit seven or eight points, though, and we won handily enough: our first championship win since 1992, my first ever.

It helped to have a win under our belt before playing Tipperary in the Munster semi-final. A packed Páirc Uí Chaoimh, ferocious game, the ball flying everywhere (so much pulling on the ball, when you look back on it) – Flynner was very good for us the same day. He went in to full-forward, threw off the helmet, and we got on a roll, scoring into the Blackrock End. I got a few points in the second half and the whole team really grew into it in that second half. I remember Dan in particular getting a great score towards the end and it was really the sign that we had won.

He won the ball, cut into the middle and popped it over (then he gave us a glimpse of his dancing skills there on the field, a horror show we never let him forget).

In a lot of ways that game is almost forgotten but it was the championship win that set us on our way. It was huge, because we'd be hurling into August at least.

It was emotional at the final whistle, because it proved that all the preparation, all the training, the savage sprinting around Dungarvan, the diet – they'd all being worthwhile. We were jumping around going crazy out on the field, all of us, and young as I was I could see what it meant to the likes of Billy O'Sullivan and Fra, who had been great servants and warriors for Waterford. That they were playing in a Munster final was a huge reward for them and Seán Cullinane.

Even when we went back to the Imperial that evening the Waterford supporters gave us a standing ovation as we walked in the door: different stuff.

It was our first significant win in years and we knew we were on the road; it was also a huge victory for the team because we had focused on that game, and on getting a result out of it. We'd given ourselves that goal to meet, and we'd met it.

It helped, of course, that we were all looking forward to it. By that I mean it was a game that I was really excited about rather than being nervous; if anything I had a tendency to get overexcited in those days before games, which could affect your performance. It wasn't nerves per se, but you could leave some of your energy behind you if you got overexcited. In that game it wasn't a sense of intimidation, though – the crowds, the opposition, the venue didn't matter.

The hurling revolution was underway and finally we could feel that we were part of it.

It helped that Roy was also on the panel, pushing hard for a starting place. He helped me in the lead up to those games – usually on the Saturday one of the lads who was driving would bring us all for a spin to get away from the build-up; we might hit for Tramore or go for a walk to chill out. This was before Facebook or Twitter: if nobody called for you, then tough. You were stuck home alone.

The match routine was pretty similar in those days. The eastern players would get together at the Granville Hotel down on the quay and head in the team bus, down to Dungarvan to collect the western lads. For games in Cork we went to St Finbarr's usually, Gerald's club, for a pre-game puck around and to get players relaxed before heading on to the Páirc.

Then came the sign that you were really playing championship: the garda motorcyclists arrived and put on the sirens and the flashers, and then you knew it. The big game. You got on the bus and looked out at the bikes leading the way, the bus nosing its way through the crowds, the people roaring in at you . . . That got the blood pumping.

In Páirc Uí Chaoimh, then, everybody knew the dressing rooms were very small, too small to prepare a team properly, so Gerald would bring us up to the gym in the stadium to give the final few words before the throw-in.

That could be a surreal scene – the takings from the turnstiles might be getting counted in one corner, a couple of the players could be peeing in a bucket in another corner, and maybe twenty players bouncing up and down with nerves, ready to go, hopping from foot to foot in the middle of the floor.

Gerald was excellent in that context: he had been in those precise circumstances so many times in a long career as a player, and then as a manager with Cork. He had all that experience of different games, different contexts to draw upon at a point in time when we were novices. The big game environment was new to us: even if some of us had had minor and under 21 success this was a different scenario. The Big Show.

The pressure was on both teams because at that point it was straight knockout and you were gone for the year if you were a point behind at the final whistle. Gerald hit the right note, however, in preparing us. The key is that he was aware of what was at stake for everybody but he didn't put us under pressure to perform. Shane Aherne was also very good but as physical trainer we probably associated his voice with the suffering we'd all been through out in Tramore; Gerald really created that dressing room environment, that will to excel.

Looking back now, the experience was full on.

———

A close, warm day, crammed into that gym, Gerald firing you up – then down the stairs and out through the tunnel under the stand in the park, the hum of the crowd all around you.

Literally. People who were never there may not know that there was an open corridor between the dressing rooms and the pitch entrance, which meant when you went out to play, you came through the people milling around beneath the stands looking for a place to sit.

Usually the guards would push them apart and create a tunnel of sorts, a corridor for you to go through to reach the field, but as you passed the people they often reached out and slapped you on the back to encourage you.

It was gladiatorial: you were a foot away from people you recognised, faces looming in, people screaming and then off you went into the arena. Usually there would be a crash barrier across the pitch entrance and for players who were psyched up to the last that could be a tricky negotiation: some just went clear out over it, out in the fresh air and the sunlight. You'd blast a ball up into the terrace, never to be seen again, and bang: you were ready.

It was all new to us, the run-in to the Munster final. The build-up, the focus, the attention . . . I can remember getting calls to do interviews and that was all new territory for me – and for all the lads.

God knows what I was saying in those interviews. It's probably just as well they've been lost to posterity. I can remember meeting one journalist for a chat in Paddy Brown's and for my lunch I had a plate of food that probably rose twelve inches off the table; he had to wait for me to push away the mountain of grub before the interview. He was probably sweating I'd have to go back to work and he'd only get five minutes of my deepest thoughts when I had eaten my lunch.

It was fun for the most part: a photographer called to our house and took a picture there, all of us boys and my dad. That was how innocent it all was compared to nowadays. The fun element. Stuff you could enjoy.

Getting better known . . . that was obvious. If you were playing for Waterford people knew who you were. As for my actual performance I thought I had only been okay against Tipperary, that I'd had a second half but that there was more in me. Because of that I was looking forward to the Munster final. Anyway, hadn't I enjoyed my own on Seánie McMahon earlier in the spring?

Clare were the kingpins. They were the reigning All-Ireland champions and some of their players had seen half a dozen Munster finals at that point.

We were an unknown quantity, really. They may have taken us for granted a little in the run-up to that game; certainly the way the game went they seemed to realise they were in a battle late enough in the proceedings.

In that 1998 Munster final Brian Greene picked up Jamesie O'Connor. Greener was our fastest player. Unbelievably fit, in great shape. He and Jamesie had a savage battle and at one stage Jamesie got past him with the ball, and I never saw anything like it.

The two of them were like two hares flying down along the side of the New Stand; Greener got back to him, close enough to get a tackle in, and Jamesie got away from him again, cut in and flicked the ball over the bar.

I remember distinctly thinking, in the middle of that game, big and all as it was, 'That was unbelievable.' It was top-end senior hurling, right there in front of you.

Clare had plenty of quality and plenty of experience to draw on, too. It was a wet day, dank and miserable. Seánie didn't hit a lot of ball and neither did I, which is always a better outcome for the defender.

We were there or thereabouts at the break but in the second half we had the wind, and Anthony Kirwan hit a terrific goal. The breeze, the goal . . . it was all going our way. You could feel it. I remember being moved out of the centre to wing-forward on Liam Doyle – another top-class defender, a pure hurler – and as the game wound down it all fell on Flynner, and the free with the last puck of the game.

People still remember those few moments. Flynn standing over the ball, a hundred yards from the Clare goal. It would have been an unbelievable score if he'd put it over, a shot to nothing – but he was the one player you'd have said, 'Yeah, he'll do it.' He was on form, he'd done well and he was confident.

I was standing near the goal, and when he struck it I could see he'd made a good connection, that it had the length but it tailed just wide right at the end. The breeze was going that way, and it just took the ball wide of the post. He was so far out that he had to give it absolutely everything and hope it went over.

Looking back, God knows what would have happened if he'd scored. The lads who'd soldiered for years would have collected a medal, but the kids like myself, twenty-odd, we could have gone well off the rails.

It was an anticlimax, the final whistle. We had a lot of positives – Flynner had done well, so had Tony, and Kirwan came off the field with 2-1 scored off Brian Lohan. But a draw is always disappointing.

I was a bit pissed off with myself, too. I felt there was more in me. The mood was good in the dressing room, certainly, we were positive about the replay.

I felt I broke even, more or less, with Seánie McMahon in the Munster final, but that disappointed me hugely. I remember sitting on the wall down by Bowe's in Thurles after the game and being not only disappointed, but visibly disappointed.

Gerald was going past and he noticed me, and he was very good.

'What's wrong with you?' he said to me. 'You're after breaking even with Seánie McMahon in a Munster final, cop yourself on. You're expecting too much from yourself, stop that.'

A bizarre scene, really – thousands upon thousands of Waterford fans walking around, a lot of them drinking from large bottles, and Gerald giving me a pep talk. But he was right.

As a centre-back Seánie was very, very hard to get past. Very strong, long arms, attacking the ball . . . if he got ahead of you with the ball you couldn't get around him. A very fair player – he didn't talk on the field, certainly.

(I didn't talk much myself either, only maybe towards the end of my career, when I knew I was getting to the end. My father would have always drilled into us that you never had to worry about the fella mouthing off, it was the quiet fella you had to keep an eye on. When I started mouthing myself late on, I knew I was getting towards the end.)

They were tough, aggressive – Baker, Lynch, strong men. I wouldn't say they were dirty; they reminded me more of the Kilkenny team at their peak, when they'd stand down on top of you for a ball and go through you.

That year the Tour de France was going through Ireland, and it was to pass through Waterford on its way around the southeast the day after the Munster final. We all took a day off and went down the town to see it going past, but we didn't realise that the best place to see the Tour de France is sitting on your couch with the television on.

'Well Ken, how will ye do next week?'

'Ah good, hopefully. Look, here's the Tour.'

Bang, bang bang. There goes the Tour.

The whole quay thronged, balloons and flags on every lamppost, and the cyclists were gone through in a second and a half. If the Munster final was an anticlimax on the Sunday, that was nothing to the Tour the following day. We shrugged and headed off to Egan's for a glass of Lucozade.

There was a lot made of the replay, and the fighting. There was a lot going on off the ball, and Micheal White and Brian Lohan had a dust-up, but they probably got sent off that day because of what was going on all over the field.

Clare tore into us, as they were entitled to do. The week leading up to the replay a lot of the plaudits had gone our way. People had said Gerald had stood up to Ger Loughnane on the sideline, people said we'd bullied Clare (bullied Baker and Lynch and Lohan? I wasn't so sure.) Clare were seasoned and had clearly said, 'We're not going to let that happen the second time.'

People reacted to it, but I didn't think it was over the top for the most part. That was the game then – you laid down a marker and stood up for yourself, because if you didn't your man would stand down on top of you. Colin Lynch went over the top with Tony at the very start but I didn't see that at the time; I only clocked that later on, when I saw the game on television. At the time I wasn't thinking, 'God this game is vicious.' There was a bit more body-checking, maybe, the intensity was higher from them and Loughnane probably had that drilled into them – but I didn't think it was carnage.

For me the game was similar to the first day, myself and Seánie more or less cancelled each other out (years later on an All-Star trip Seánie went along with that diagnosis, by the way).

Looking back now, I was only twenty, so it wasn't that bad a performance, but they got a cheap enough goal from a long-range free, and after that Niall Gilligan stuck a good goal – he gave Landers the eyes and put it away well. That was it. They were too experienced to let that slip, and they didn't, and we had a long last quarter listening to the Clare fans enjoy the ride to the final whistle.

We were poor in the second half. End of. Their big players were good, that was the difference – Jamesie was good, Lynch, Frank Lohan. Alan Markham was good.

What made it worse was that the losers had a week to turn it around for the All-Ireland quarter-final against Galway, who were an experienced side then. And we were playing in Croke Park: that had been the aim at the start of the year, to make it there, but it was a daunting prospect after two full-on encounters on back-to-back Sundays, then, to head out again a week later and do the business.

We trained hard enough that week, oddly enough. We took it easy early in the week and Gerald, again, was very good. He reminded us how close we'd been, that we were so near. We trained on the Thursday and headed for Dublin on the Saturday.

Dublin: different straight away, the entire experience. We overnighted, for instance, in the Berkeley Court Hotel, which we regarded as Dublin 4, really sophisticated. Saturday evening we went in to Croke Park.

This was in the middle of the rebuilding – the Cusack Stand was new, the terraces were in place, the Hogan Stand was still there, and we were clambering all over the place until Gerald called us in. We weren't allowed to head out pucking around on the surface with hurleys and sliotars, but he sent us onto the field and put us in our positions, where we'd be lining out the following day.

That was a good move. We were pretending to hit the ball, but it was definitely worth something to us to go there, to see the place from the players' perspective.

After that we headed off to Shelbourne Park and the dogs. More novelty. We laid a few bets and relaxed, and it sank in that this was the way it was done by the successful counties, the weekend experience, if you like.

For the game the following day our focus was simple: we'd laid it out at the beginning of the season that we wanted to play in Croke Park, and now we had that opportunity – none of us had ever played there as seniors and we felt we had a chance to go a stage further. It was a beautiful day, Offaly beat Antrim handy in the curtain-raiser, and we went out to take on Galway.

I was marking Padraig Kelly, a good hurler, but I'd had two poor games and my pride was stung: no matter what happened I was determined to show what I could do. I hadn't played up to scratch so I said I'd have a cut.

I'd been going well early in the year and that day in Croke Park went well for me too. I got points in the first half, I fielded the ball, I carried it – the surroundings and the occasion had no impact on me, at times I felt like I was on my own in Walsh Park, hitting the ball over at my ease.

We hammered Galway: 1-20 to 0-10. Sean Daly started, got a goal, everyone was flying – Tony was putting over sideline cuts, Dan was everywhere. Having lost the replay the week before, to have that kind of experience on your first visit to Croke Park was unforgettable. Not all our visits to Croke Park went as well, but you could enjoy the last ten minutes that day.

Or at least you could if you didn't twist your ankle. That was the only thing: I won a ball around the half-back line and went forward before popping off a pass, and I went over on my ankle. I knew I was in a bit of bother, but in the rush of winning a game in Croke Park – Waterford, winning a senior championship game in Croke Park – I didn't feel too worried.

Gerald thought of another master stroke on the way home. We were heading off down the coast road back to Waterford when he got the bus to pull over and he headed into an off-licence, himself and Greg Fives and Shane Aherne.

———

Out and back onto the bus, the three lads with slabs of beer.

And Gerald made everyone take a couple of cans, and everyone had to sing a song – it was terrific. That's what makes the whole thing, that sense of being together. We rolled on down the coast road, singing away – Hartley probably giving us 'Ambrosia' all the way down – and on to Muldoon's when we landed back home.

A win, a trip, the crack you'd have: that might only happen a few times in your life, that experience. You wouldn't have it even once a season. But when it does happen, you know it's special, and again, it was Gerald who knew how to do that.

That was Sunday, and on the Monday we had a meeting. In the All-Ireland semi-final it was Kilkenny, and we were confident.

It wasn't the Kilkenny of later years. It was pre-Cody. Henry Shefflin wasn't on the team. They were good, they were still Kilkenny – the neighbours who'd had it over us for so long – but we felt we had a good chance.

We prepared well, we had the same regime we had before the Galway game, but the hype was different. It was the first Kilkenny–Waterford game in the championship since 1963, the counties are right next to each other, there are so many Kilkenny people working in Waterford . . . there was a lot of interest from outside the country, from the media and so on, but again, you'd notice the difference between the pre-social media era and now. If you saw someone you saw someone, grand, you'd chat away, slag each other – but that was that. The pressure wasn't building all the time thanks to the phone in your pocket carrying messages and posts and tweets from all over the country.

Which isn't to say the buzz wasn't building. One evening there was an event over in Ferrybank, a pub gig, and RTE sent down a camera crew for it. If you're from Waterford – or Kilkenny – you'd know that Ferrybank is border country. Disputed territory. Some of the houses are Kilkenny, some Waterford.

Half of it is within the Waterford county boundary, and some in Kilkenny, and the population's split fifty-fifty. The boundary between the counties isn't that clear-cut, so if you wanted to row in behind whoever was winning there's no one going to correct you at passport control.

You walk down from Ferrybank, cross the bridge and you're in the heart of Waterford city, it's that close. The atmosphere would have been fantastic there in the couple of weeks leading into that game.

We thought we were ready, and we were. We went to Inchydoney in west Cork for a training weekend ahead of the game, and we played a challenge game. I was trying to get my ankle right and was desperate to play in it – a beautiful day, lovely pitch, and a good few locals after drifting out to check the new kids on the block, a team on the rise.

I missed around ten days of training, and got back the week before the Kilkenny game, but it definitely affected me, those lost ten days. I wasn't as good as I'd been against Galway, certainly.

The day of the match I had the ankle strapped, a dose of Difene – a sign of things to come, maybe – and I picked up Mick Kavanagh, who was in his first year.

In the second half I went into centre-forward, and I contributed. I was better than I'd been in the Munster finals, but I didn't have the influence I wanted, or the influence I'd have on games in later years.

It was one we left after us. Even now it torments me to think about it. In my time the 2002–7 side we had was the best team I played on, but people would say it to me even now that that year was our best chance of an All-Ireland.

It was 1-11 to 1-10: scrappy. Their goal . . . D.J. mishit a free, we blocked it, Niall Moloney pulled and Brian Flannery nearly got a hurley to it. That never happens. D.J. not striking the ball properly, the ball breaking just the right way?

That was the cushion they got and they rode that to the end. I hit four wides myself, and two in particular I should have scored. I'd gone in centre-forward, where I always felt more comfortable because you could pull away either left or right; with those two shots I'd pulled away and just rushed my shot a tiny bit. Wide. Wide. Two of them in a row. That'd haunt you.

Tony got a goal – he picked up Hurler of the Year that season, well deserved – and we got it back to a point, but when we launched our last attack, Pat O'Neill collected the ball. Over.

It was devastation. As low as you'd get. We were so together – we were like a club team, just playing for the county – after the NuTron, the weekends away, the matches, the sacrifices, the support we had, the atmosphere was building all that year – even the Tour de France, brief as it was – and we were thinking we'd done everything right.

You'd nearly have to be dragged off the pitch. My uncle Declan was the PRO at the time and he brought me off the field. You'd feel almost physically sick. In one way it's hard to describe, but on the other hand we were to see so many semi-finals that you'd think I'd be well able to describe it.

The thing about 1998 is that it was relatively open. Kilkenny weren't as strong as they became. Cork and Tipperary weren't at their best. Offaly were in the final and were a good team but we would have had lads who'd won All-Ireland U21 medals against them a few years earlier.

They'd had their own saga with Clare, Jimmy Cooney blowing up early and so on, and all of that contributed to the sense of a really extraordinary season, a glamorous year for hurling.

And we were one of the stories of that year. People still recall it, and it meant something to us that we were a big part of that season.

I got an All-Star nomination. Ten of us got the nod, and we had a good night at the ceremony, but I didn't deserve an award. I knew that. But I also knew there was more in me, that I was better than I'd shown during the year. I was only twenty. I knew I'd improve.

Mount Sion won the county title that year, which was a bright spot – our first title since 1994. I was still suffering with the ankle but couldn't get it sorted out, as I felt I had to keep playing. We lost to St Joseph's in the Munster club championship but I was getting tired. In that year's U21 county title, for instance, I was poor. It had been a few years since I'd had a break, but given how much we'd gotten out of 1998, I couldn't wait for 1999.

We didn't go training after the league as hard that year, and it showed. We didn't get the same results, and we probably weren't putting in the same effort. The training was very hard, but was everyone sticking to the NuTron diet as rigidly as the year before? I don't know.

We'd gone to the Canaries in January, and fellas had weight on them. It was obvious. All of us did, which wouldn't have been unheard of at that time for players after Christmas, but it showed the little change in attitude. Fellas were keen to get back training but it meant we were catching up all through the league.

By the time we played Limerick in the championship we were on track. I marked Dave Clarke and got four points, but Flynn was very good at full-forward on Brian Begley. We won but it was a tough game. Limerick had beaten us in the championship as recently as 1997, so when we won we felt 'We're timing it right for later in the summer, for these games – we don't have to be right for April.' Cork next, and while they'd beaten us in the previous year's league final we were confident.

And when we heard their team we were even more confident. We trained in Thurles a couple of nights before the match and on the way home their team was announced over the radio: six debutants. A load of young lads.

I remember thinking in the car, 'We're grand, we're better than that Cork team.' We all felt the same in the car: confident. Another Munster final on the horizon.

The day of the game, of course, was the start of that Cork team. Tony wasn't right that season, he was struggling with an injury all that year, and he was under pressure having won Hurler of the Year the previous season. On the surface everything looked fine – Tom Feeney eating broccoli before any other player had heard of it, meticulous with his weights, Fergal Hartley was flying, Flannery going well – but we were well beaten.

Cork's debutants were flying – Mickey O'Connell, who scored half a dozen points, and Timmy McCarthy, who hit four points himself. We thought we'd handle them.

Flynn got a goal late on and we were in the hunt, but we were short a few percentage points compared to the previous year. Not much, but enough: maybe the preparation being off slightly came against us, but whatever the reason, we lost and we were out.

It was such a downer after the previous year. After all the progress, it felt like we were back at the starting line all over again. I had five points from play – and a fine cut on the face, six or seven stitches' worth – so I felt I'd contributed.

1998 had been up and down for me, but I had nine points in two championship games in 1999. I was 21 and felt I was learning more in every game, I was more confident and less inclined to question myself.

The fact that it was Cork wasn't significant for Gerald in 1999. He was very good in the dressing room, and this was a time when a lot of the pre-game stuff was based on aggression and getting guys hyped up. Not nastiness, just making sure lads were well primed.

He was very good to talk to guys individually, to prepare them for specific challenges, and to speak to the team as a whole. He never made it about himself; we made it about him in Limerick in 2001, because we felt he'd be gone if we lost, and I felt he was uncomfortable with that.

He was emotional because of it, and we were emotional

because of it, because he'd given everything to us for those years. I'll never forget the gym in Páirc Uí Chaoimh in 2001 – that's where we had to speak, not the dressing room – and when things went wrong between him and the Cork players a few years later I was devastated for him personally. I don't know the ins and outs of that but he'd done so much for so many of our players outside the game, let alone as a coach, he was like a father figure.

He advised lads on jobs; if a player was a student he made sure he had a couple of bob for a drink if we were celebrating; if someone had to take time off work he'd insist that he be looked after by the county board. Stuff we'd never have considered, but he was well on top of it.

Gerald was the reason Waterford have been at the top table since 1998. It might sound over the top, but he's the one who changed all of that. All the players would agree that he set the standards in terms of professionalism, the standards that everyone had to reach.

Before that we had good players, good club teams, but we were on the periphery. He changed all of that. For instance, coming over to me after the 1998 Munster final when I felt I hadn't played well: telling me to grow up and not to be expecting a nine out of ten performance every time I played.

Before that I'd be unrealistic, I'd be pissed off if I didn't have a big game every time, which was ridiculous. That was a good lesson to get, sitting on the bridge by Bowe's and Gerald telling me to cop myself on. I never forgot that.

That time the Monday after the game was nearly always a downer, to be honest. Young and single, no kids, the whole year builds to the Sunday, you're obsessed, the game is on – then it's over. What next?

———

That's why I'd take that Monday off work. It was nothing to do with going out drinking, but it was just to try to deal with the aftermath and try to relax.

You're in such a bubble with the team, training so much, spending all that time together, talking in a group, week-ends away, planning as a group, working on the plans together.

Then it's gone. You're out of the championship, say, walking off the field with the crowds gone and it's over. And it's close enough to depression. That's why you need the balance. On the Sunday of the game, even if you lose, you're with the lads, you go out, but at least everyone's together.

Then you wake up on the Monday. Where to now? It's hard to face reality.

(Even when I tried to play the system I'd feck it up. I remember after losing to Clare in 2002 I went to the doctor for a cert for a few days off, but I made such a bags of coming up with an excuse that he sent me to Ardkeen for blood tests. I met one of the lads from Mount Sion out there, and he said, 'You're after training for six months, you never looked better,' but I ended up losing a whole day getting blood tests when all I wanted was a few days off.)

Despite losing to Cork, I still had that confidence. We played Tipp in the U21 championship and we were three goals down but we hit three goals late on to get back into it. I got two: I was flying it.

Even though the team made more progress in 1998, the boost that 1999 gave me in my own development was huge. 1998 was brilliant, one of my favourite years because it was such a roller coaster, and it was our first year of big matches, big occasions, big wins, and back to Waterford after then – Muldoon's – thinking we were great fellas.

But I got more out of 1999. In that year's county final though, there was murder. We played Ballygunner and it was like an out-take from *Braveheart*.

Roy got a red card for messing off the ball and I hit the keeper, and a fight started. Roy came back on and hit someone, and it all kicked off.

The following day we all met up and went for a jar and the paper was passed around – there was a picture on the front of the row, with a garda in the middle, his hat falling off, and we were saying, 'Oh-oh.' We ended the year with a title, the U21 county. It was my last under-age game and I got ten points when we beat a combination of Tallow and Shamrocks, Eoin Murphy and James Murray and the lads.

For me it was a good year, and I was keen to build on it for the following season. I'd only be playing senior and I was mad for it.

As it turned out, 2000 was a continuation of 1999. I was flying. We played Cork in the league in Walsh Park, and they were All-Ireland champions, but Brian Corcoran was moved off me.

I got a score that day – Micheal White played the ball to me as I was coming diagonally across the field and I flicked it up and struck it over the bar without handling it, one of the best scores I ever got.

When he was moved off me it proved to me that I'd progressed from 1998, for instance, when I'd marked him first. I felt strong and fit. We got to the league semi-final and I got five or six points. Motoring. I couldn't wait for the championship against Tipperary.

Tipp had Philly Maher making his debut at full-back and Gerald said to me, 'Go in on top of him, he's starting off and won't fancy marking you.'

I was named at centre-forward so it was a surprise to Philly when I landed in on him, I could see that. The first ball, I went out to the wing, fouled: free and a point. The next ball went to the other wing, I got it and pointed it.

Jogging back in I was thinking, 'I'll go to town here.' Now Philly Maher became a fantastic full-back, but every player starts somewhere, and I felt he was vulnerable if they could get the ball into me. I was full of confidence.

A few minutes later I was going for the ball, just about to catch it – and I got a slight nudge in the side. I came down on my ankle. Desperate pain: I couldn't get off the ground.

Gerald and the physio came out and I was saying, 'I'm in bother,' and they were saying, 'Ah, you'll be grand.'

I'd gone right over on it, my full weight, but I asked them to strap me up. I went back into full-forward and said, 'Forget it, this is knockout, if we lose we're gone.' The next ball I went for it, turned Philly and put it over the bar. Great stuff.

The ball after that, though, my ankle went again. I couldn't get up. The lads came out and told me to try to get through to half-time, and I managed one more point before the break.

In the dressing room they injected the ankle but I couldn't move. Couldn't go at all. I ended up getting taken off with quarter of an hour to go, and we lost by a goal. Our plan was to get the ball in fast to the full-forward line, and when I went off the plan went too.

My father had had his hip done that year and was on the

sideline with my brother Pat and I remember looking at them and feeling I'd let them down, almost. I wasn't aware of what I'd done at that stage, but I couldn't walk.

That night we went out in Waterford of course. Pub and disco instead of hospital and X-ray. The next morning when I saw my ankle, though, it had swollen up, black and blue from the shin down.

I rang Donie Ormonde, who's a radiologist in the hospital, and he said to come out. Walking into Ardkeen my father – who'd just had his hip done, remember – was too fast for me; I had to ask him to slow down, which suggested I was in big trouble.

It was the usual Monday after losing a championship game; on the Saturday everything's great and the songs on the radio are the sweetest. On the Monday you feel like putting the radio out the window when you hear the same song. That Monday I felt even worse, and when Dr Tadhg O'Sullivan saw the scan he said, 'You're in trouble. Come back to me tomorrow.'

I'd torn everything in the ankle – all that was holding it together was skin. Every ligament around my ankle. Of course, I was saying to my father, 'I told you it was sore,' and he was saying, 'I said nothing.'

I had the operation. Cast for the summer. Out for the year.

I was captain of the club, and we'd been slated after the big fight in the previous year's county final, we were determined to set that right, and when Tadhg said I was out for the season it was a fair blow.

In fairness, Nicky English was managing Tipp at the time and he rang me in the hospital, which was a classy touch.

This was before everybody had a mobile, so he had to do some work to find me – to ring the hospital, the ward, all that (of course Nicky is married to a Waterford woman, so . . .)

I was off work as well that summer. I'd been working in Teve, a grand handy factory job, but Derek McGrath's dad, Nicky, was leaving Rentokil to take over a shop, and he said to me, 'My job's coming up because I'm leaving, they'll be looking for someone to take over. The hurling is going well for you, you're well known, it's ideal for you – car, mobile phone, all of that.'

I wasn't sure but Nicky had the customers built up, I thought about it and said I'd do it, but a few things soon convinced me otherwise.

For one thing I couldn't drive. I had a rep's job but couldn't drive a car. My father had me driving two hours a day for a couple of weeks, trying to learn. Every day. Starting, taking off, the gears, the whole thing.

And then I got a notion: where are they going to give me this company car? If they give me the keys outside the office I could end up driving it through the windows.

Anyway, they gave me the car up in Limerick, about five in the evening. I was staying up in Limerick for job training so the rep who was training me brought me off to this car park, threw me the keys and said, 'Follow me.'

Rush hour. The Ballysimon Road, one of the busiest roads in Limerick. Christ.

He took off, flew down the road, and I just couldn't catch up with him. Sweat patches under my arms with the stress: what's going on? Rang my father and said there was a funny light flashing on the dashboard.

———

'Check your handbrake,' he said.

I was trying to catch up with this guy with the handbrake half up.

The stress didn't end there. I sweated as much trying to get in and out of a multi-storey car park in Limerick, and then I had to point the car towards Waterford. To this day I'm not sure how I got back; I aged about five years between Limerick and Cahir alone.

As the rep I'd get calls and go out to check what was involved. A chap rang once and said he had wasps, so I went out to see. He had a huge shed out in his back garden and he opened the door; when I looked in every wasp from three counties was buzzing in a big heap up in the corner.

I slammed the door shut.

'Whoa, you've wasps all right,' I said. I nearly got a weakness.

I'd be afraid of my life of rats, say, and going in around factories looking for them . . . I knew it didn't suit me. By rights I should have gone back to Teve, but I didn't. And in fairness to Rentokil, they were very good to me when I did my ankle against Tipperary.

I was on crutches for weeks, going to matches, but around August I'd had enough of it. They took the cast off and I got a moon boot, and I started testing myself. The county final was on early but I felt I had a chance of making it. I'm a pretty good healer and it was tempting to try to make it.

Tadhg was a Ballygunner man but he's been brilliant to me over the years, always, and he said, 'Chance it – I think you're okay, you're not going to damage it.' We had a challenge up in Clonmel and Kevin Ryan was our manager. He threw me on in the second half and said to take it easy, but sure as soon as I was on I ran around like mad, as usual. I got a couple of points and felt I was bad.

I trained for a couple of weeks before the county final, and we won 1-20 to 0-9. Roy and Eoin had been suspended after the previous year, and they were excellent, even if Roy did this weird dance when he won a free in the second half, but we were all obsessed with winning that game.

We got a psychologist in the previous week, for instance, and he was very good, getting us to discuss how we felt we were being viewed – that we weren't tramps, that we were ordinary decent GAA people. And it worked really well, coming out of that room I felt confident we'd win.

Ballygunner had it over us. We hadn't beaten them in a senior final but we were very good. Eoin Kelly got five points for us from midfield, Anthony Kirwan hit four points, Tony was very good – the adrenaline got me through. The ankle was fine during the game but I was in bits afterwards. My experience helped me, but the leg wasn't too healthy after it.

Being the captain and getting the cup, having been told I wouldn't play again that year. . . I remember sitting in the club with Eoin and Roy having a pint and saying we needed it as a family, as a club. My father has seven county medals, and we needed to get going.

As a club we'd always try to show respect, we'd always provide players to county teams. We have more county titles than anyone else, though, and sometimes we'd detect an anti-Mount Sion feeling, maybe, because of that. In 2000 we said 'Feck that, we'll fight hard for this one.' No one was going to stop us.

It's hard to describe what winning a county means if

you're not part of a club. You all meet up back at the club and you see fellas you mightn't see from one end of the year to the other, but you're all together, the cup is there . . . it's as good a feeling as you'd have anywhere. Someone sings the club song, and lads are standing on tables singing along. It's a good year's work.

We probably took it for granted that time, we were flying with the club. Now if we won a county Dawn mightn't see me for a week: the celebrations would demand it.

Turning into 2001 we probably knew the end was coming for Gerald. He'd been there for a few years and I certainly was listening to him as intently as ever, and I couldn't point at others who weren't, but it's difficult for any manager to keep it going when you're not winning.

We'd been to the Munster final, to League finals, and we knew 2001 was going to be a watershed. The likes of Seán Cullinane and Stephen Frampton were pushing on; there was a sense of now or never.

(Frampton. In the 1995 county final against Ballygunner Jamie, my cousin, got a very good goal for us early on. He was eighteen, I was seventeen, the two of us high enough for the game. Wound up.

Frampton was coming outfield against me after we got the goal and I hit him a shoulder going past.

'Stop,' he said, 'You're too young for that, now.'

I felt terrible. He was right. I was running around half-embarrassed for the next five minutes, copping myself on. A few months later he was picking me up for county training. I had great time for him, he was tough as nails and he'd think his way through games, and just the way he looked at me

———

after I did it . . . I could have been sent to the embarrassment-bin for a few minutes after it.)

In 2001 I had a broken thumb early on, and because of that I did savage training on my own: the sandhill run out in Tramore, sprints around the club field, three-quarter pace runs. Running, running, running.

I got very fit, and once the thumb started to heal I was so eager I fell in for the drills one-handed. Swinging the hurley, keeping up. I was the captain. I was eager.

We played Limerick in Páirc Uí Chaoimh, and their supporters . . . the Limerick support is always mental. Singing, roaring, flares, the whole thing. Always. They bring a fantastic atmosphere to it.

Gerald didn't say, 'Look, I'm gone if we don't win here today.' He didn't have to. We knew it. I felt that after all the years, after everything he'd done for us, we owed him – for what he'd done for the game in the county.

And in the gym in Cork we were well wound up. Lads catching fellas by the chest, players nearly crying. That's how it was, you were winding fellas up to go out through the door, nearly.

It worked, too. We got eleven points of a lead, playing unbelievable stuff. It was Mullane's first year, he was very good, and we were 2-7 to 0-1 ahead.

The same problems kicked in. If it were Cork or Kilkenny they'd have gone twenty points up, but Limerick came back at us. Ollie Moran got a goal before half-time to keep them in it, and in the second half we just kept giving goals away. Three of them, and all through our own mistakes. Their crowd got behind them, they were rolling . . . People give out about

Páirc Uí Chaoimh and the dressing rooms, and they were small, but how long are you in there putting your gear on? That wouldn't bother me. The showers are cold? You'll live. The minors are showering next to you and there's a fog and the sweat is rolling off you, you're bursting to get out onto the field.

And it was a cauldron. However it was built, the stands came up around you, a brilliant surface and the crowd was in on top of you. And that day was typical, roasting hot, huge crowd, great atmosphere.

I got a few points and that was something, but in the dressing room the feeling was clear. We'd let Gerald down. To go that far ahead, we shouldn't have lost; he had us hurling well but we couldn't close it out. It was an absolute and utter sickener.

I gave up Rentokil later that summer. We were dumped out of the club championship by Lismore, so I felt it might be a chance to do a bit of travelling. Padraig Hayes, one of my best mates, was in Munich, so I said I'd head over to him, but I got a call from the States. Would I be interested in coming over to play?

I'd been to the States before, a flying visit, and I was thinking I'd head over, then get back to Ireland before hitting Munich for the Oktoberfest. Perfect. Myself and Seamus Prendergast hit for New York and we stayed in Woodlawn. Great crack, loads of Irish around, a few pints. Lovely.

Up the next morning and down to Gaelic Park. I had no helmet, ran around grand in the one-hundred-degree heat. Poor Seamus had the full mask and helmet and I'd say the Budweiser was coming out through the pores on his face. He got the blame for overdoing it, when he'd be one of the most conscientious players I ever lined out with. Honest as the day is long.

Later that summer we headed over for another game; myself, Henry Shefflin and James Murray. Landed on the Friday, couple of drinks, then on the Saturday down around Manhattan for the sights – Henry joined up with us, so we saw Central Park, the Empire State Building, all of that.

Murray and myself were in one of the horse-drawn carriages fluting around and one of the other carriages pulled up next to us: 'Well Ken, who are you playing for tomorrow?'

Played the game the following day in Gaelic Park – Limerick, who had Ciarán Carey, Mark Foley and a couple of others. I was on Carey, running everywhere, pulling on everything, a tough day in the heat. We lost by a couple of points.

The cans came out, then up the road to an Irish pub in the Bronx for some food, and the following day all the players met up again. We said, 'Whatever we have we'll spend, we'll have a right good day of it in Manhattan' – myself, Murray, Henry, a few more. Great day, and because a couple of the lads knew the city, they brought us to some great spots. Not a care in the world.

We were down around the meat-packing district at one stage, I remember looking up at the skyscrapers. We ended up going to a disco off Times Square – the Copper's of New York, a place just to keep the night going. We told all and sundry we were in the chorus line from *Riverdance*, and Henry, in fairness, put on the moves to convince the audience: danced away like a good thing. I told them I couldn't because of insurance issues and got away with it.

91

We crashed with one of the lads' pals in Manhattan, and got up the next day hunting breakfast. We thought Times Square would be a place you'd get pancakes but when we landed there it was deserted.

The date was September 11th, 2001.

One of the gang got a phone call and we realised something was up when we saw the screens with the news in Times Square showing what was happening a couple of miles south of us. We were only four or five miles away from the World Trade Centre and soon enough people started to walk past covered in dust from the towers. We were queuing up to use payphones; I got through to the mother and was trying to explain to her that New York wasn't the same size as Waterford, that we were safe where we were, but in fairness they didn't know where we were for a few hours.

The announcements started then, that Manhattan was going to be shut down so we headed for the train back to Yonkers, where we were staying, and the train was jam-packed. Thousands on it. That brought it home to us a bit, the seriousness of the situation.

When we got to Yonkers we realised we were missing Murray, but we found him soon enough ('Ye're alive,' was all he could say). We got to McLean Avenue in Yonkers and everyone was in the pubs watching the news – lads in their construction gear – and it began to sink in, the sheer enormity of what had happened.

We were supposed to fly out that Tuesday evening, but obviously that wasn't going to happen: the airports were shut down. We decided to head to the beach so we caught a bus going that way; the beach was closed, though we only found that out when we got off the bus.

We were stuck there for ten days, all in all. Every day you'd head off to find out what the story was with the airport – still closed – and in fairness to the club which flew us out – Waterford – they looked after us. They gave us money for food, though we ended up spending that on pizza and beer, mostly. P.J. (from Kerry) and Jimmy Duggan (from Tipperary) made sure we weren't short, to give them their due.

Another guy, Mike Prendergast from Tallow, brought us down to a firehouse the Saturday after 9/11. Mike had been a fireman for twenty years and because the lads were working such long hours, he was going in to make them dinner, and he told us to come along.

We headed off with him to Harlem, to the firehouse, and it was up on the notice board – 'Mike Prendergast cooking dinner tonight' – and he made cheeseburgers and corned beef for them. They gave us a tour of the firehouse, and it was an eye-opener, to see them heading out on calls after the week they'd had. We went to a memorial in Gaelic Park then, the following day.

We were young, and it probably didn't sink in, really, the enormity of what had happened, but it was a time and a place you couldn't forget.

Myself and Peter Queally went off to play for Munster late in 2001 and Paddy Joe Ryan, who was with the Waterford County Board, was involved with Munster as well.

We were talking, the three of us, about who'd come in to replace Gerald, and we couldn't wait to see who it'd be. It was a little different to nowadays, when there's half a dozen names – and usually the same names – thrown around as managerial replacements no matter where the vacancy is.

There was a meeting in Lawlors Hotel in Dungarvan where we were introduced to the new manager, Justin McCarthy.

Justin had a great reputation, but we wouldn't have known him that well – YouTube wasn't an option for us to do research at that time – and for a lot of the players, like me, Gerald was the only manager we'd known at intercounty level. We were probably set in our ways, used to what we were doing.

But Justin spoke very well, in fairness. He referred to it being a fresh start, which it was. No pre-Christmas training. We all fell back in for January 2002.

The difference between them? Justin was all hurling, all the time, and there certainly wouldn't have been the same emphasis on savage physical training.

But that's what we were used to, and as a result it probably took us a while to buy into what he was doing, what he believed in. He kept saying to us, 'You'll be grand in the summer', but we didn't have Shiner Aherne putting us through cruelty, running around out in Tramore. We weren't sure, and it all came to a head after a national league game against Dublin up in Parnell Park.

Bank Holiday Monday, around Easter, and Dublin beat us well. We were shocking.

There was a blowout in the dressing room after that. Harsh words. Flannery, Queally – who was always a brilliant driving force, a guy who'd give everything and someone people always listened to – myself: we all spoke up, as did others, and we said it wasn't good enough. There was murder, to be honest. We weren't happy, but Justin wasn't panicking. That was his mantra, that we'd be fine come the summer.

We stopped in the Poitin Stil for grub on the way home from the Dublin game, and fellas were still grumbling, still unhappy. Was this progress, getting a hammering in Parnell Park?

It's gas when you look back at it. At some of the sessions Justin would have us working our wrists for ten minutes. No ball at all. And fellas looking at each other a little embarrassed, thinking, 'We're senior hurlers, what's all this about, pulling on an imaginary ball?'

That took a while to buy into. Clearly Justin wanted us to improve the speed of our hurling, so that we'd be flying when it came around.

It didn't help that he was more stand-offish than Gerald had been; he wasn't looking to be your friend. It was business and you were there to train and to improve. That was a new approach to us and I'm sure our ways were new to him.

There were a couple of green shoots soon enough. We beat Galway in the league at Walsh Park, for instance, and they'd been in the All-Ireland final the previous September. That told us we weren't too far off getting it right, maybe. We played Clare in our last league game to try to qualify for the knockout stages, and they beat us, but only by a point.

That was another good sign, but only to us. It didn't look that great from the outside. Some of the local papers were writing that we didn't look fit, for instance, and Ger Loughnane said after the Clare game that neither team would do anything that year.

Then, though, the clock went forward. The ground got

harder, the evenings brighter. Justin took over the training totally and we started to click. We went to Antrim a couple of weeks before the championship and it was brilliant. A turning point.

We hammered Antrim out the gate in a challenge game – a decent crowd there to see it, a fine sunny day – and we made a weekend of it. Saw the sights, had a few jars, and on the way down on the train the feeling was good.

I remember distinctly on the train from Belfast to Dublin, thinking, 'We're grand here. We're fine,' and everyone else thought the same. The whole thing had clicked. The season had turned.

One thing Justin brought in was that really close attention to detail, particularly your hurley. I wasn't that way inclined. I remember one time playing an U21 game and using a hurley I found in a skip (I'd say Justin would get a weakness if he knew that).

As far as I was concerned, if the hurley I had was heavy and thick that was fine by me. I used Wexford hurleys for years, then I used O'Brien hurleys from Tipp, before I went over to Flanagan's. But whatever I had, Justin would take the hurley off home and fix it up, and when you'd get it back you'd find it strange for a while, but whatever he'd do to it would always improve your play.

I think he realised himself fairly early that he had a team of hurlers, and sometimes at training the sliotar was fairly zipping around, the standard was excellent. I always had a good relationship with him – though I always got my game, which will keep your relationship with any manager on an even keel – and he always urged players to express themselves.

He had decent players coming through, too. Eoin Kelly was coming on the scene, and he was unbelievable. Our Eoin came in, it was Mullane's second year, Eoin Murphy and Seamus Prendergast were establishing themselves.

Looking back now, incidentally, people mightn't remember that Justin often used Dave Bennett as a sweeper, long before anybody else was doing that, though he didn't have the massed defence to go along with it. Generally it was an era of individual combat, one-on-one battles, and that suited us as a team by and large.

Fellas skipped into training after the trip to Antrim. The spirit was great, and there was the confidence in the team that you get when everyone is positive about where the team is going.

Good vibes all the way until we played Dublin in a challenge in Thurles two weeks before the championship. I was flying the same evening, went in to hit someone with a shoulder – and I popped the AC joint.

Going home that evening in the car, I knew I was in trouble. I'd been playing centre-forward and was a key man in our plans, and I was gone: ten days to the championship and I was out. I didn't hit a ball between that Dublin challenge and the day of the championship game against Cork. The day before the game I had a run around the pitch in Mount Sion, trying to get ready to some extent.

I went with the team to Thurles for the game, or more exactly, to a specific location within the town. This was another twist Justin brought; we'd go to the clerical training college there before the game for a cup of tea and a sandwich.

Quick chat, puck a ball around – there might be fifty thousand in the Square, a few yards away, but you were grand and secluded within the college.

(When I see those gates now if I'm in Thurles it all comes back – the nerves, the anticipation. The excitement.)

A couple of nights before that, though, Justin would have gone through that Cork team and compared it to our team: he'd have gone through us both as teams, player for player, talked about who each guy was marking, and he said we were better than them, that we'd beat them. And the players believed him, after all we'd done.

We were written off by most people, given the way the league had gone. And it was a huge game for us as a team, because it could all have gone either way. Losing in 1999, 2000, 2001 . . . things hadn't been going our way. It was hard to make an argument that we'd improved upon the 1998 season at all.

But it was a different team. There were new faces – Kelly, Murphy, our Eoin, Mullane – and Justin said we'd out-hurl them. It was business, pure and simple – the fact that he was from Cork never came into it. He never raised it and we never mentioned it (we'd had a Cork accent so long we could understand what he was saying fairly well). In that sense, looking back, it was seamless – Justin and Gerald were of an age, similar enough outlook, successful.

On the way up to the stadium, then, on the bus, I was next to Flannery. He said, 'We're going to win.'

I said, 'We are, I hope I'm okay to play if I go in.'

Doc Higgins, who was our team doctor for years, gave me an injection in the clerical college before we went up – I nearly passed out when I saw the weapon he took out to

inject me with – and he told me it'd kick in within the hour. Grand.

The day was terrible, wet and windy, and the game was poor enough. Cork got a goal through Eamonn Collins but we hung in there. Holding on.

I wasn't expected on but they sent me to warm up early on and the crowd were roaring in at me. I was thinking, 'Jesus, I'd better do something if I get on here.'

Mullane got a great score just before I went in with just twenty-two minutes gone – centre-forward on John Browne. Diarmuid O'Sullivan came to test the shoulder as soon as I went in, but I saw him coming. And side-stepped.

The shoulder was perfect when the injection kicked in: good as new. And I was bursting with confidence. I'd been nominated for an All-Star three years in a row; I was twenty-four but the seasons were slipping away at the same time. I wanted to make an impression. I hadn't had a great run-in to the game, but out on the field, I was ready.

Fellas were confident at half-time; we knew there was plenty left in us. Tony got a vital score for us in the second half from miles out the field – he let fly, the ball bounced in front of Cusack and slipped past him. Goal.

That nudged us ahead, but Cork stayed in touch. Tough, tough, Munster hurling. I was holding my own and we had our noses in front until the last minute, thirty seconds, and bang, Cork got a point to level it. Damn.

Then Queally got a ball and even though – like myself – he'd have a tendency to pump the ball in high, he found Brian Greene down the wing with a great ball. Greener was only just back from the States, on the panel a few weeks, but he won the ball, cut inside and found me with a great handpass.

I had a simple enough chance, and I tapped it over. If I'd missed it I'd have been sick, it was a chance any player worth his salt would have scored, but I was delighted. Lost the head a bit, ran around with the hands up to celebrate (Hartley said to me afterwards, 'Mac, they could have gotten an equaliser while you were running around like Christy Ring.')

We stopped two more attacks from them before the final whistle. A win, and a ticket to another Munster final.

There was huge relief. We hadn't been in a final in four years, and there was a sense of 'Will we ever get back there' creeping in, a worry that we wouldn't, or couldn't, kick on. It was one of the great victories we had because of that, even though people mightn't remember it that clearly given the way the Munster final went.

I missed the first couple of nights' training back after the Cork game, then I was back. Fully fit.

Justin was so full of confidence that he took all of the hype in his stride, the build-up to a Munster final, whereas we were cock-a-hoop. Full of the joys. He was the one saying to us, 'I told ye it'd be fine for summer, ye'd be grand,' and we were thinking 'Yeah, this guy's a guru, he knows every-thing.' True believers.

I was working in Arkopharma in the stores. I was on two different shifts but I never missed a training session. Every-thing was flying until the Thursday before the Munster final, and another minor mishap.

One of the lads rolled over my toes in a forklift.

I had steel toecaps on my boots, so I was steeped. I was a little nervous heading to Walsh Park that evening in case I couldn't run – on the way up I was saying to myself, 'You're years waiting for another Munster final and you won't be able to budge, you're jinxed.'

I was grand, though. And in a way the incident took my mind off the occasion. I was so concerned about whether my foot would be okay or not that the nerves drifted away. So getting rolled over by a forklift was a blessing in disguise.

Justin played a couple of good cards in the run-in to the game. He got Frankie Walsh and Martin Óg Morrissey from the great Waterford team of the fifties and sixties to come in to us and have a quick chat a few nights before the final.

We'd finished training with backs and forwards and the ball had been absolutely flying around. Zipping it. And after that, one of those evenings the last week, Frankie and Martin Óg were there on the sideline.

They just said, 'Lads, ye're there on merit, enjoy it, it's four years since a lot of ye were there but ye have to take these games and not let them get away from ye; enjoy it and hurl to your ability.'

It was a nice touch and took the pressure off. Not that there was a lot on us anyway. It's a cliché for a player to say after a win that nobody gave his team a chance before the game, but *nobody* gave us a chance against Tipperary.

Babs Keating had said in one of the papers that the crowd would be gone home at half-time, not that we took any notice of that kind of talk. In a general sense my view was always that a pundit's opinion was just that, one man's opinion, and if you had your work done and were confident then that stuff didn't matter.

But in fairness, that would have been the general view. Tipperary were the reigning All-Ireland champions, they were on track to make more progress in 2002 and they'd beaten Limerick well in the other semi-final.

Our routine was pretty similar for the Munster final compared to the semi-final, and would be the template for future years, particularly Justin's dissection of the opposition.

He often went down the middle – talk about the opposition's full-forward, centre-back, about getting at them. For Tipp that year he caught them by putting James Murray out on Tommy Dunne, who was Tipperary's main man. An absolutely brilliant hurler, but if you could hold Tommy then you'd be confident of doing well against Tipp.

Justin's plan was for Murray to do the sticking and Tony to do the striking in the middle of the field. The team was well balanced – Fergal Hartley was flying at centre-back, with Queally and Greener either side, Stevie Brenner in goal was reaching us in the half-forward line with his puck-outs, putting us on the attack straight away . . . that was a huge plus, it made things a lot easier for us up front, and we had the players to exploit that. Eoin, Mullane, Flynn, Kelly roaming: we had quality to punish them.

It was another desperate day, wet, miserable, cold, not related to what you wanted in a Munster final: too wet for a puck-around before the game. Instead of going to Midleton's pitch to warm up we ended up going to the hall to loosen out. I remember saying, 'What kind of a day is this at all,' and Justin said, 'Don't mind that, ye're grand, ye're ready.'

He was right. No one was nervous. For a Munster final, there was no pressure. I didn't feel any pressure, certainly, and 1998 was a massive help in that you knew what to expect.

I put myself under a certain amount of pressure to perform – 'You're going well, you need to do it now today, you're twenty-four' – but it wasn't a stress coming on from outside or a pressure you couldn't deal with. I remember being comfortable with it; my thinking was, 'You've been working towards this your whole life, this is the day.'

Justin put me in full-forward on Philly Maher early on, but I wasn't really in the game for the first quarter of an hour. Getting tetchy.

As a team we were well in touch but I needed to get involved, to get on the ball. Moved out to centre-forward. Great.

The first ball that came in I fielded and laid off for a score, and I was on my way. Seamus gave me a good pass and I hit a point. Eoin was cutting through the middle and got pulled down: Flynn buried a goal. Kelly was causing havoc, Mullane hit a brilliant score.

It was all going to plan, but we were also conceding goals. Tipperary's Eoin Kelly was doing damage, but we hit three points in about a minute before the break and were only a point behind at half-time.

I couldn't wait to get back out. I'd scored two points and had been involved in the game, everybody was positive, everyone was encouraging. On some days that happens: you can sense it in the team, everyone believes, everyone is committed to it. There might be fifty thousand in the stands but there's no more pressure than if you were playing a challenge.

Tipp didn't give in: we hit points and then Stevie landed the ball inside their 20-metre line and Tony, ghosting in, pulled first-time and got a great goal (fantastic celebration too, robbed from *Match of the Day*).

They got a couple of goals, Benny Dunne was very good for them, but we took over. I felt like I'd win every ball I went for, and the game went my way. I wasn't thinking I was great, more 'This is what you should be doing, drive it on'.

We were never ten points ahead, so it wasn't like you could coast through the game, but we took over towards the end. Dave Bennett hit a great point from the wing late on, and he was shouting at us coming out. I was shouting back at him. I'd played with him under age, and we'd had some grim outings, but not that day. I got a point then, my fifth of the second half, and I knew we were nearly there.

With about a minute and a half left Murray gave away a free in the middle of the field, and I ate him; I remember him looking at me as if to say, 'Mac, would you relax.' At that stage we were there. We knew we had it won, and all we wanted was the final whistle, and eventually we heard it.

The Munster final doesn't mean as much now, but back then it was nearly forty years since we'd won it. I was on my own in the middle of the field and I just fell to my knees.

You don't feel it'll happen, you've lost a couple, it's so long since the county's won . . . we didn't know what to do. We hardly knew how to celebrate. We ended up doing a lap of honour before Hartley even collected the cup. There were stewards coming over saying, 'Lads, come over for the cup,' and we were thinking, 'Oh yeah, right.'

The crowd went wild. Literally. Eoin got up on the wire and hugged Clive Power and Colin Morrissey, buddies of his, I saw my father in the covered stand. It was great, actually, to just walk around the pitch without people hanging off you. The whole thing could sink in.

We went back to the stand for the presentation and the Tipperary end was empty, and someone said, 'I thought the crowd would be gone from half-time, not full-time,' and then we got the cup. And we went on another lap of honour. Why not?

Nicky English came into our dressing room. I knew him from the All-Star trip the previous year, when I was the only Waterford man there. His wife's from Waterford and they kind of took me under their wing, and when he came into us he was very gracious, very sincere. I'd have great time for him. He gave a great speech, and it added to the occasion.

We went over to the Imperial Hotel for some food, and then on the way back to Waterford we had one of the most memorable adventures we ever had.

Anyone who's driven the road from Cork to Waterford will know the bridge outside Youghal that takes you into Waterford. As we were going back they stopped the bus on that bridge and we walked across it, all the players with the cup.

(Because we did that, a regularly scheduled Bus Eireann service had to wait on the far side. I'd love to know what they thought of the nutcases walking across the bridge drinking bottles of Coors, holding a big cup over their heads. Every time we pass the bridge in the car I say to Dawn, 'Did I ever tell you about the time we walked the cup across the bridge?' 'Only every time we cross over it.')

We heard there were crowds in Dungarvan, but it didn't sink in until we got there. We had nothing to judge it against. When we got there we were put up on a flatbed truck in the main square of the town, facing a sea of people.

Hartley said to me up there, 'You got man of the match.' I didn't even think about that: 'Ah grand, yeah.'

We went on and had a crazy night. Didn't make it to Waterford, half an hour down the road: we stayed in the Park Hotel and went rampaging around Dungarvan like . . . like pirates.

And then, on the Monday, we had an open-topped bus around Waterford itself. We'd all agreed to meet up on the Monday, the team, and we toured the quay and into the plaza on the quay.

Looking back, it seems a bit crazy to have done the two days, a bit over the top, but we were waiting forty years for it. At that point it was like an All-Ireland. Up on the bus, lads were saying, 'This is the life,' thousands waving up at us. Fantastic.

And a couple of lads had done well out of the win, too. Two of them backed Ronaldo to be top scorer in the World Cup – which was finishing the Sunday we played the Munster final – backed Brazil to win the World Cup, and backed us to win the Munster final.

They made a fortune off it, too, but I'd say it was all gone by Monday night the way they were spending it.

We had a mayoral reception, and I was winding down. I'd be like that – if I was happy enough with how the game had gone, happy after a couple of bottles, then I'd slip away, and that Monday I had enough of it about half eight in the evening.

(I did the same for years after county finals with the club. We'd be out for a drink on the Monday, and I'd love it, but I'd warn the rest of them, 'I'll be home for *Coronation Street*,' and I would be, sitting down with chips and the telly. Steaming, but at home.)

———

I was in work that Tuesday, the two-to-ten shift, and afterwards I had a few with Feeney, Flannery, Tony and a few more in Nicky's and up in the club, and then hitting town – and that was it, really. Three nights out. We were back training in Aglish on the Friday.

That might be where things started going a little bit wrong. That first session, for instance, was an open session, and it was mobbed. We went to the local pub afterwards for grub, and it was chaos.

So it was a full week before we got it all out of our system, and every session after that . . . people found out where we were training, and there was a crowd scene nearly every evening. Didn't help.

There were other distractions. I got a couple of awards, and I'd always have prided myself on being able to refocus, but it was tricky. I remember marking Murray a few times in training, and I got narky with him a couple of times when I shouldn't have. He was marking me tight, which he was supposed to be doing, and that always brought me on, but then when I got odd with him I remember wondering myself why I was so touchy.

We worked hard but some of the territory was new to us. The night before we played Clare we stayed in the Citywest Hotel in Dublin, and I didn't sleep properly at all. Too excited altogether.

I remember saying to Tony, who was rooming with me, 'Are you asleep?' which is never a good sign for either man in the room.

Getting up the next morning there was a sense of 'Yes, I got through the night,' rather than being refreshed after a good

---

night's sleep, and a few of the lads were saying the same when we went for a stroll around the hotel.

Maybe it was getting on top of us; that can happen. A couple of other little things went against us – the bus driver got the turn into Croke Park wrong, for instance, and we had to ask a steward for directions to park.

Fellas were getting tetchy about it – 'It's not this way, it's that way,' – and as we were pulling in, the Clare bus went in ahead of us and you could see them rubbing their hands, almost, with a touch of, 'We have these lads, sure they don't even know the way into the stadium.' They were seasoned – McMahon, Lynch, Gilligan, the Lohans, plenty of players with All-Ireland medals. Bags of experience.

When we eventually got out onto the field I had nothing in my legs. I was on Seánie McMahon and I got a decent point in the first half off my left, but at one stage I was going for a ball out on the wing, and I should have made it, but Lohan beat me to it and came out the field with it, banished it down the field. I was left thinking, 'What the hell is going on?'

At half-time I said to Shay Fitz, our physio, that I had no energy. I was down about it. I asked for a rub on my legs to try and get going.

A lot of us started the game well and fell away. Queally had a ball in his hand and might have cleared it but Clare turned it over and worked the ball into Alan Markham, and his goal gave them all the momentum facing into the closing stages of the game.

And that was a disaster for us. Claustrophobic. They outfought us, outmuscled us, and out-hurled us. It was as bad a thirty-five minutes as the All-Ireland final in 2008. We were poor as a unit and poor as individuals.

I hit three poor, poor wides in that half, and we never clicked. And then I had the incident with Gerry Quinn.

In the second half I was moved out to wing-forward on him. Gerry was an abrasive enough player, fast, aggressive, he was having a good season with Clare. Having a cut.

I was waiting for one ball and I got the handle of the hurley in the back, and I said, 'Hey, don't do that again.' Then I got the handle of the hurley into the back again and I saw red: I let fly and pulled behind me, full force.

He must have been holding his hands up because I caught him right on the hand, but I didn't see where I made contact with him. I looked and he was down on the ground and I went over and said to him, 'I fucking told you.'

I lost the plot. I was having a nightmare of a game, I'd built the whole occasion up in my mind for so long – years, really – and I shouldn't have done it. I don't think I even hit the ball after that, my head was gone. I have a good recall of games normally, but the rest of that is a blur, apart from feeling sick to my stomach walking off the field.

It had been a massive adventure and you just didn't want it to end, but sitting in the dressing room afterwards, I couldn't believe it. The year was over. I wasn't thinking about what had happened with Quinn, I was more embarrassed by how we'd played. By my own performance.

Heading up in the lift to the players' lounge, Colin Lynch and Brian Lohan joined me, and I got the impression they were looking at me and it sank in a bit.

Then upstairs one of the lads said Quinn had gone to

hospital, that his hand was broken. At that stage I was looking out the window over the Dublin skyline and thinking that was another year gone, another semi-final lost, but it wasn't long before I was thinking of other things.

We met up in Waterford for a drink the following day, and the whole thing exploded: Gerry Quinn had been struck off the ball and everybody knew who had done it and what was going to happen and it was terrible . . .

I was sitting with the lads thinking, 'What'll I do here – admit that I did it?' My attitude was straightforward: basically, that if that's how you play you have to expect it back every now and again. That's how I played and when I got it back my attitude was, well, what goes around comes around.

One report said the dogs in the street knew who had done it, and the others were barking at me in the pub, which didn't help the concentration.

You're having a drink but you've lost and the season is over: the environment is false. Top of the world on Sunday morning, you lose the game, give a poor display, break a player's hand . . . what do you do?

I probably didn't handle it properly. I don't remember getting any advice from the county board, for instance, and I settled on a selfish course of action, if you like. I wanted to play for the club, because we had a great chance of a county title, so I said nothing.

It wasn't the right thing to do then and it's not the right thing now, looking back. I regret it. What I did I did in the heat of the moment, that was probably in me, but I regret not coming forward afterwards.

I was sick that he'd miss the All-Ireland final: I might have lost my temper for a second but I certainly didn't want to do a player out of that opportunity. I was happy he made it back and that he played well, though obviously it wasn't great preparation for him. He never said who'd done it, either, though he could have.

I tried to put it out of my mind and went back to the club. At the All-Stars I met him in 2002 but we didn't talk at all. There was plenty of grief for me for a while afterwards – we went to the All-Ireland Sevens that year out in Kilmacud, for instance, and one lad up there must have an iron throat, he spent the whole day screaming 'McGrath, you tramp' at me. I eventually went over to the crowd where he was and called him out, but no sign.

I deserved it. If you're a Clare person and someone busted one of your player's hands then you'd be cross enough. It was a horrible time, but you can't ignore what I did. I didn't have any time for someone giving me the hurley in the back, and I went over the top with my response, but I was glad he made it to the All-Ireland final.

For us the whole year was a learning curve. We had to learn how to deal with that, being Munster champions: the expectation, the celebrations, all of that. Clare had been waiting for us. They beat Galway by a point – Colin Lynch hit a terrific winner that day – and they'd been through the mill, they knew just what to expect and how to prepare.

Back with the club the rhythm was different. At around that time we headed up to O'Loughlin Gaels in Kilkenny for a game, a beautiful Friday evening. Kilkenny were having their press night for the All-Ireland final, and from

O'Loughlin's we could see all the cars parked in the Nowlan Park car park.

On the way back home we stopped off in Knocktopher for a pint; myself, Flannery and Tony.

'I'm going back to Kilkenny,' said Flannery.

'Right, we'll head back,' we said.

We weren't prepared for a night out in Kilkenny, really, but we improvised. Tony didn't have shoes so Flannery loaned him these deck shoes which . . . (see, Flannery's title as the worst-dressed man in Waterford has never really been challenged: huge American football tops, shocking flares. Wicked, really.)

All that night in Langton's we gave Tony dog's abuse over the deck shoes and going over the bridge in Kilkenny he accepted they were terrible.

'Give them to me,' I said, and I threw them into the river.

That left Tony shoeless in Kilkenny, but the following morning he tiptoed to Dunnes and got flip-flops. We said we'd have one pint and get the train back home, but one led to another. All day, going through the cycle of great crack to heads wrecked back to great crack and so on.

We woke up the next morning. Panic. We were playing Gowran in a challenge, so I got a taxi from Kilkenny to Waterford for the game. I was in bits. I ended up getting the winning point, somehow, but Jim Greene, who was the manager, knew there was something going on.

The next night we rolled into training he ate us in front of the whole squad: 'This is disgraceful, ye're on the beer for two days and we're trying to win a county. I know ye're down after losing to Clare, but cop yourselves on.' Made a show of us.

But it worked out. After that it was grand. I got past the

loss totally after Greener gave out to us and settled down to focus on the club.

Now he'd told us he was going to do it. We had to say sorry in front of everybody, the whole thing, but after we trained we watched Dublin play Armagh in the All-Ireland football semi-final, and when Ray Cosgrove missed the free with the last kick of the game to draw it, we felt, 'Well, they're like us now, time to move on.'

(Disclosure: of course, Flannery never stopped complaining about his shoes, and eventually I gave him a few bob for them. I can't remember if I told him they were lost in a mercy drowning or not.)

We won the county final and I ended up getting twelve or thirteen points. We had a good run in Munster. A good win over Adare, who had Mark Foley at centre-back, a good win over Mullinahone, who were without Paul Kelly and lost Eoin Kelly through injury, and a good win over Sixmilebridge in the final – they'd beaten us in the 2000 final. So we got the Waterford loss out of our system, and it all turned around after Greener's lecture.

It was probably the most important winter I ever had, to have that. We had the All-Stars on the Friday of the Munster final and it was pretty tight security that time, you wouldn't know if you had won or not. We were all kept backstage at the ceremony and they were announcing the winners live, but Brian Lohan came over and told me I'd won one at wing-forward. (I was more impressed that Lohan wasn't coming over to kill me after the Quinn incident.)

First All-Star, but early to bed and back to Waterford the following morning. Up to the club that Saturday – a terrible day, December 1st – but I stayed there hitting frees until I was refocused on the game.

That night, then, I went out to visit my grandfather, Jackie, with the All-Star award. He loved it when we were going well; he'd be in Brady's having a pint or two, talking about his grandkids. He was allowed to have two or three pints but if we won the county, say, he'd go to the club and have four, maybe wobble a bit. My mother would be giving out to him but he'd wink at us: 'I only had two.'

A character. He passed away the following February, so it was great to get out to him with the award.

We dug out a great performance against Sixmilebridge to win in terrible conditions, twelve points to ten. Haulie White got three points, I got nine. One of the sweetest we ever won.

I picked up one of the Chaplins and the day went my way. Because we'd lost to Clare in the All-Ireland semi-final I put myself under pressure to do well against another Clare team that day: I had myself convinced they were saying 'This fella isn't as good as people say he is'. We celebrated that win, and because myself and Eoin Kelly had won All-Stars as well, there were plenty of reasons to celebrate, but the club was the main thing.

It was one of the greatest wins Mount Sion ever had, and showed what the club means: heart, courage, honesty, team-work, never giving in . . . I rank it as one of the best wins of my career, and to see one of my best mates, John Cleere, go and lift the cup was unreal. The clubhouse rocked that night like it never rocked before.

We trained hard in January, prepared well, but Dunloy were better than us. The easy thing to say is that we were complacent, coming up against an Antrim team, but we weren't, honestly.

We knew they were a very solid team, we just felt if we played up to our standards we'd beat them. We maybe misjudged the winter break a little, I felt a bit leggy after a full year and a half's training, not quite as sharp as I'd like to be, but they had a man in front of me and one behind – no space.

I tried hard but I only got one point from play. They'd done their homework but we missed goals and points – John Meaney blasted one shot off the goalkeeper's head and it rebounded back out the field – and it became a game we just weren't going to win. Flannery won a great ball very late in the day but the referee blew him up for over-carrying and they tapped the free over the bar: a one-point win.

Back to the gloom, and it's nearly worse because it's your club. First club semi-final, and it's gone. When we got back to the clubhouse, then, we noticed immediately something was up. The atmosphere was all wrong.

'What's up?'

'Larry Quinn. He died of an aneurysm.'

Larry was involved in the underage section, an official in the club for years – he'd died suddenly. Fellas went home immediately, and the defeat, disappointing as it was, was put into perspective immediately. We were preparing to go to his funeral soon afterwards rather than getting downhearted over a hurling game.

The bad news didn't stop there. Not long afterwards I was selected as Munster Hurler of the Year but my grandfather Jackie died unexpectedly at that time. Jim Greene brought me up to the ceremony but I was miles away. The national league started up that weekend and I said I'd play – Kilkenny in Walsh Park – but I wasn't focused.

A couple of weeks after that I got sent off for pulling in the air against Galway. I pulled, Diarmuid Cloonan gave me a kick when I was on the ground and the referee gave both of us a red card. Gone for three months.

I had to go to Croke Park for a hearing, which I found hard to believe. At that point I'd been pulling on the ball in the air all my life – everyone did it, to keep the ball moving past you – so I was stunned by the three months they wanted to give me.

I'd lost the All-Ireland semi-final with the club, then the county, I'd had the Gerry Quinn thing hanging over me and my grandfather had passed away and now I was looking at a three-month suspension. The whole season, more or less.

At the hearing I said, 'That's my game; if I have to stop doing that then I might as well give up hurling. That's what people want to see.'

Now, it didn't look terrific when they slowed down the video and played the clip over and over – in fact I was hoping they'd stop playing it, because it looked worse every time it came on – but they saw sense and gave us a month each eventually. Missed a few league games.

That didn't help my preparations. We got over Kerry, beat Limerick in a replay and got to a Munster final against Cork.

Thurles, packed to the rafters, sunshine: the Munster final. Setanta, Tom Kenny, Ronan Curran. It was Curran's first year, and he wasn't the Ronan Curran he would become. I had collected the man of the match award in the previous Munster final so I fancied my chances.

I was on the ball and got chances, but I hit seven wides over the seventy minutes. Seven points in 2002, seven wides twelve months later. A nightmare, and all the worse because I was actually involved in the game. I was moved from centre-forward to centre-field for the second half and I must have fielded seven or eight puck-outs.

How close the margins are: most of the wides were wide by a foot or less, I'd say.

Mullane was very good – three goals, and the salute to the Cork support, and we were seven up at one stage. Setanta got a goal to bring them back into it but we were in control. It turned on one play – Paul O'Brien got a shove from Mark Prendergast, who didn't play that much for Cork, but he won a good ball that day, lifted it in on top of Joe Deane, who caught it over Brian Greene and finished it, cute as a fox. Goal.

Cork won by four or five in the end. An anticlimax. I got plenty of criticism, though I never minded hitting wides, to be honest; it would have been worse, to me, if I wasn't hitting any wides, or wasn't involved. I was in the middle of the action, though I wasn't putting the ball over the bar, and I was getting fitter and faster all the time.

We got Wexford in the qualifiers, and I was flying again: five points in the first half off Declan Ruth. Motoring. Mullane was banging points over.

They pulled Larry Murphy outfield, though, to create space in front of Paul Codd: he got a goal and the old failings resurfaced. We couldn't hold them out. Mullane got a knock in the eye, I got crowded out, maybe we should have moved someone out to follow Larry . . . the game ran away from us and the season was over early enough.

You're left there thinking, 'Was last year a flash in the pan?'

We were in control in that game, though. Mullane and myself got ten points from play, and you'd feel any team scoring that would be able to get over the line. In fairness to Wexford, they drew with Cork in the All-Ireland semi-final, they had plenty of quality themselves, lads with All-Ireland medals from 1996 – Larry O'Gorman, Adrian Fenlon, all of them.

4

ONE DAY IN JULY: 2004

In January 2004 I had a knee operation, a posterior ligament in my knee needed some attention, and when I got back we were playing Limerick in the second tier of league games. After playing my entire senior career up front with Waterford, I was wing-back.

People probably thought Justin was keeping things fresh just for the league, but he'd already told me they were thinking of moving me there. 'Ease your way into it,' he said, 'you'll love it there.'

And I did. I'd always had a hankering to play there after being a centre-back underage, my father had played there, and I enjoyed it. We beat Limerick and the next day I was wing-back again, marking Timmy McCarthy in Cork, where he ran me from start to finish. I was thinking, 'How am I going to catch this guy,' but I settled eventually.

Then we played Tipp up in Thurles, and we had to avoid losing to make the final, and we drew. The game went well for me, and I was getting settled there. Facing the ball I got a new lease of life; I was twenty-six and it felt like starting all over.

Justin brought Gerry Fitzpatrick in to do the physical training, Seamie Hannon and Nicky Cashin were on board as well, so there was a freshness that year, a new set-up.

And that applied to me, too. Justin probably saw that I needed something new and that I was going a bit stale in the forwards; I had the best years of my career in the backs, and that mightn't have happened if I'd stayed up front. It was the best move ever for me, in all honesty.

For all that, we were desperate in the league final against Galway. We were playing in Limerick, which we never liked anyway, and the atmosphere was dead, our timing was slightly off with our warm-ups . . . there weren't many positives in it, but Dan got a goal and a few points. It was the start of a great year for him.

(The game wasn't as good for Eoin, who ended up at corner-back on Damien Hayes. We found out that Eoin wasn't a corner-back, anyway.)

We went back training the week before we played Clare and we tore lumps out of each other, and I remember seeing Justin laughing to himself on the sideline. I don't know if he'd planned to peak for Clare in the championship, I don't think anyone would throw a league final, but . . .

He told me I'd be centre-back against Clare, and in training I was picking up Brick Walsh in those games. Great preparation, because we hammered into each other. He was a huge addition to the panel, and we were very alike in terms of our outlook: we spent years moaning and complaining in car parks before and after training. The football background helped him with fielding in particular, but his hurling sharpened hugely over the years.

We were completely focused on that game. It was Clare, we wanted to improve our results against them, Justin was ready, and we knew that within that week, after the league final, we'd turned it around.

After the throw-in I got the first ball and banged it into Mullane, he put it over the bar, and you could tell from the reaction of the team that we were up for it. There was a small shemozzle and we all piled in as a team: someone said, 'Ye won't be bullying us today.' Another small sign, but they all add up.

Colin Lynch was marking me, and he was one of my favourite players – determined, aggressive, tore into it fully always, but he wasn't a centre-forward. I caught the ball, I was wound up, and I knew I was on form. I must have been on the ball thirty-odd times in the game; it was one of the best days I ever had in a Waterford jersey.

I put myself under pressure to do it against Clare, that was a big motivation for me after 2002, but it was a day you'd back yourself for every ball, to win every tackle.

And it was the day Dan took off. He got his first championship goal and scored another two on top of that for good measure. Fantastic. The team were on fire, but it was a bit of a freak performance, because Clare were a good team.

I saw Anthony Daly standing on the sideline that day, his first outing as a manager in the championship, and now that I'm managing Mount Sion I have more sympathy for him. I know well that you can have a day when it all goes wrong for you – the team have trained properly, the warm-up is going well, but it just doesn't happen.

Our lads hit the ground running, though, and winning a championship game by nineteen points . . . it was only May, but it set us up for the year, to have won a game in Munster by that number. We had a good night to celebrate but the lads skipped back into training. They were mad to get into it all over again.

It was huge after the collapse in the league final, when people might have been doubting us – and Justin, maybe, though he'd probably have said he planned it all.

We got closer to him over the years. In 2003 we'd gone on a holiday to Morocco. He picked it, and for a man into photography like him it was probably great, the scenery and so on, but the rest of us were stuck looking at camels. I wouldn't be in a rush to go back there.

But he relaxed a bit on that trip, chatted away and even sang a few songs. He didn't drink, but he mixed in. We came to know his moods – when to approach him at training and when to leave him alone.

And, as I say, when you're playing, your relationship with the manager is always good. He'd have tried to get the most out of me, and I appreciated that. I never made it up to the ball alley he uses in Cork, though a few of the lads did and they felt it improved them.

The weights programme went well, too – our first. Gerry Fitzpatrick came up with it. We'd go to the Waterford Crystal gym and it was fantastic: in one game early on I remember catching a couple of lads with shoulders and felt I was at my ease, really strong.

It was a full hour's circuit, twice a week, and I followed it religiously. We were up in Colligan one day training and when I took my shirt off Gerry said to me, 'Look at yourself, you're cut, you're getting really fit.'

I'd never heard that expression before, and when I found out what it was I knew well that I wasn't cut, but that was Gerry's gift, he'd make you feel good about yourself; I bounced out to training that Sunday morning. Gerry lectures in psychology in WIT and he knew how to keep everybody's spirits up, how to keep you going.

He was a great addition to the back-room team, maybe the best; he had a great way about him, and was a good conduit for dealing with Justin. We're all still close to him.

I stuck to the gym programme over the whole year and from then on, really. And in fairness, you'd have to say that was Justin changing his approach from 2002, say, when we hadn't done as much physical work. He gave Gerry a free rein that year and we benefited hugely.

Now there were other years when he didn't give Gerry that freedom, which was a pity. We were always bang on, just right for games, when Gerry was in charge. He had us using speed bands before any other team, for instance.

We had Tipp next in 2004. Páirc Uí Chaoimh jam-packed, a scorching day and a great game. The ball was flying, we got goals . . . it was the start of the lads celebrating their goals, which got a lot of publicity. That all came about naturally, though. It just happened.

It was just a great time to be playing. I was happy at centre-back but I pulled a muscle in my side with around ten minutes to go and was in desperate pain. Had to go off.

———

We were losing at that stage, despite having played some fantastic hurling. The second half didn't take off for us – they kept us at bay, Brendan Cummins made a couple of unbelievable saves, including the famous dive to keep Flynn's shot out – but we kept going. Persevering. Looking for that one chance.

Time was almost up when Seamus Prendergast won a fantastic ball. He was always a great man to win the ball, though he'd say himself he wouldn't always give the perfect ball after that. He put a brilliant low ball into the Tipp square that time, though, and Paul O'Brien flew across and pulled first time: goal.

It was some way to end a game. My side was killing me but I legged it out with the rest of them to celebrate. A tough game and we got over the line. That was one of the most important goals we ever scored; Paul will never be forgotten in Waterford because of that.

That year's Munster final against Cork stays in a lot of people's memories. It helped us that we were used to the experience by then – it was our third in a row.

Myself and Ben O'Connor, the two captains, had a gig with Guinness the Friday week before the game – running around cones, hitting the ball for some fanzone – and the two of us were sitting on the grass chatting for half an hour there in Midleton.

The Cork lads were as experienced as us, so he was looking forward to the game as well without getting wound up about it – 'See you Sunday', and off home in the car.

But the Square in Thurles that Sunday was like nothing I'd ever seen. It was heaving. Full on. The Cork support out in force, shaking the bus as though we were Fenerbahçe going to a derby in Turkey. We were laughing our heads off, some Cork lad with a beer in one hand and giving you the finger with the other: how could you not laugh?

We had the worst possible start to the game, though. A ball bounced up into the air and Garvan McCarthy took a swipe at it. Harmless. I'd turned to run upfield for the puck-out and I heard the roar: ball in the net.

It didn't faze us; we'd been there too often for that. We had plenty of time to pull that goal back. But Cork started at lightning pace.

It was my first time picking up Niall McCarthy, the start of years of bouncing off each other like a couple of demented sea lions, and while I knew he was strong and aggressive, he was also very quick, moving from wing to wing. I always tried to mind the space and protect the full-back line, but Niall's energy made you wary. You had to track him.

Early on I tried to find Brian Phelan with a handpass but Tom Kenny nipped in and stole the ball; he took off and I went after him but his speed was frightening, he sped off and put it over the bar.

I remember thinking, 'If these fellas start running at us we're in trouble.' Brian Corcoran got two good points and we were chasing our tails, basically. I said to Tony that we had to settle things down, to slow the play a bit – which was some admission, because we'd always loved playing the game fast. But we got into it.

Dan was the difference in the first half. He was fielding the ball, hit three points in a row off John Gardiner. Eoin Kelly got a brilliant goal, cutting in along the end line and finishing from an angle.

The game was taking off. Niall was quiet, and when Eoin Murphy got a pass to me I hit a point from long range. Getting into it, hitting the ball. I wasn't dominating but I was feeling good.

Dan got a great goal when Kelly mishit the ball – he fielded it and buried it. Flynn, Mullane, they were flying.

At times you know the game is good, even if you're in the middle of it. I remember thinking at one stage in the first half, 'This is unreal.' I wasn't admiring everybody's skills, but it was obvious that if you made a mistake it was going to be punished – Cork were that good at the time, having lost an All-Ireland final the previous year.

At half-time we were a couple of points down but Justin was very positive – he pointed out that we hadn't played at all, that the game was there for us.

Going back out I stopped the players in the tunnel and said, 'Lads, we can't come off the pitch unless we win; we're good enough to win.'

Out, ball thrown in, Mullane gets a point. Great.

We won a free on the Cork puck-out, over on the wing, and I went over to take it, but before I did I could see there was a commotion at the Cork end. I heard the roaring of the crowd and then Seánie McMahon, the ref, calling Mullane out of the group of players: red card.

Shit.

For the next ten minutes they were on top; we lost our way. The crowd got behind them, they were dominating – Ronan Curran came up the left wing, popped the ball over the bar. We were hanging on by a thread.

Flynn got a couple of brilliant points to keep us in contention then, which we badly needed. Gradually we got to grips with the game in the half-back line, and started to protect the inside line. Dan won a free and Flynn had a chance of a point, but he went for goal . . .

Even now you'd think they should have stopped it. Going for goal from that range is mad, but that was Flynn. His skills were unbelievable – what he'd do at training was out of this world. If he'd had Mullane's physique or fitness he'd have been unstoppable, but he could always put the ball in your pocket.

I wasn't that shocked he tried it. In the 2002 county final against us he had a free to draw the game in the last minute, from distance, and he bounced it off the crossbar – a dipper from thirty yards. He had that confidence in his own ability, and it was well founded.

We needed that goal. We weren't going to beat them with a string of points. And the surprise knocked Cork back, too. You could hear it even from their supporters: they were shocked.

But then the game took off all over again – it probably went up another couple of levels. Unbelievable.

The last quarter of an hour was brilliant to play in. It was enjoyable, really, even though there was pressure on us. We got a free out for a Cork square ball at one stage and I remember walking outfield with my arm around Seánie McMahon, the referee; I had an arm around his shoulders and was saying, 'You're right, Seánie, you're right, that was a square ball.'

It was that kind of game, that kind of day. In 1998 I'd have been up in a heap, but that day I was mad for the ball. Loving every minute of it. Brick was winning fantastic balls for us,

Eoin gave everything, caused a bit of chaos, Seamus was a huge presence for us.

For all that they nearly caught us. A long ball dropped into our half and Kieran Murphy got it, turned, and had Ben O'Connor steaming through off the shoulder – all he had to do was pop it into his path and it was a goal, nailed-on.

Murray got a bit of a flick on the ball, it came to Deccie Prendergast, and he got it to Eoin Murphy; Murph cleared it out the field.

That was the turning point in the last quarter, because if they'd gotten another goal there was no way we'd have reeled them in. A goal into that end – the Cork end, which looked dark and red at the same time, somehow – and the momentum would have gotten them home. Seamus fielded a high ball and pointed: two up. Time running out.

Cork got one more point, worked it down the line and a score, and then it was nearly over. We were one ahead.

I hit a free and drifted over to the wing to cover; Cork cleared and I was there, I told Phelan to leave it, I picked the ball and hit it too well. The contact I made with the ball was too good, even though we were playing against the wind – and it carried past our full-forward line.

Fuck.

Wayne Sherlock got the ball for Cork, fed Ronan Curran, who probably shouldn't have cleared the ball straight down the centre, but he did. I'd gotten back into the middle and was underneath.

People said afterwards I must have noticed Diarmuid O'Sullivan nearby, winding up to pull, but I didn't. It was a stage in the match when you knew a big play was crucial, and I said to myself, 'I'm grabbing that.'

I fielded it but it wasn't over then – I tried to get past Timmy McCarthy but he stepped across me. Free.

I knew it was over. There is a photo of me swinging the hurley at this point in the game. I don't even remember doing that, just the feeling that the game was won, surely. They wouldn't get another point to tie it up. The game was safe.

And there was a sense of satisfaction, being involved in a big play at the end of a game. That's the kind of thing you'd dream of as a child, and then it happens, just like that.

I roared up into the sky, the crowd was going bananas, Tony was screaming next to me – the adrenaline was pumping then.

I threw the ball back for the free – I was blowing hard, the effort was catching up with me, and Sully said something as he passed.

I was still wound up, of course, and said, 'What did you say?'

'Some catch.'

I tapped him on the shoulder: 'Thanks, Sully.'

Flynn went for a point from the free but it dropped short, and the game was over.

It was an unbelievable finish, but then it was an unbelievable game from the start.

Playing in it, you wouldn't be taking a step back and saying, 'That's some noise', but you couldn't help noticing the roaring that day. It was deafening (the only other time I heard noise like that was in 2006, taking the free against Donal Óg in the All-Ireland semi-final.)

I shook hands with Sully at the final whistle, and I could

see the crowds swarming onto the field, and my first thoughts were: 'Where's my front teeth?'

I was the captain and I needed those for the presentation. Gerry Fitzpatrick had the teeth, though; I was presentable when I went up to get the cup.

It was all the sweeter being captain after what had happened to my father against Cork in the Munster finals of 1982 and 1983.

Cork had destroyed Waterford in those games, and even though Tipperary are the other traditional powerhouse in Munster, for Waterford people Cork are the team that gave us some unmerciful beatings, such as those two Munster finals.

After the 2004 game, then, it meant something to have won.

Those two defeats followed a lot of those Waterford players around, particularly the first one, when Cork ran up a huge score. We were in Kerry once on holidays and when my father got a couple of drinks in a pub, the barman said it came to 5-31, the score Cork got that day. Funny man.

We'd have been aware of that. We lost two Munster minor finals to Cork ourselves, they were the standard bearers, and to beat them in a Munster final in Thurles, a great game of hurling, with a man down for half the game . . . that was something we'd been crying out for, a win like that.

Justin was delighted for us too, and for himself as well, probably. He might have felt hard done by in Cork – I don't know the ins and outs of how he finished up with them – but he could take huge satisfaction in the win, and in the manner of the win.

People always say it's all about winning, and it is. But there's more to it. It's about hurling as well. It always is.

Maybe I'm old-fashioned, or out of touch, when I say that, but I believe it. I was proud to play in that Munster final – and proud to have played that Cork team, a bunch of lads we had great time for and who, I'd hope, would have good time for us – and proud to win it.

When I collected the cup I made a conscious decision not to make a massive speech. I said something along the lines of 'Hopefully this is the first one this year.'

I stumbled through the Irish – I had a couple of sentences ready, but the stewards asked me to ask the crowd to push back, there was a bit of a crush on the field, and that put me off with the Gaeilge. Just got through.

They carried me off the field, which was special. I'd never been carried off the field before, which makes it stand out even more.

Those twenty minutes or so after a game – that's a special time, one that's hard to describe. The win is just soaking in, and you're all together to enjoy it. That's more important than any individual awards.

Afterwards we walked down the town, into the Square, and into one of the pubs, Cuchulainn's.

It was mobbed and when the Cork lads saw Mullane, who was still very down after the sending-off, they started singing 'The Banks' at him to get a rise out of him.

We were at a loss – we hadn't had a drink yet, remember – but then we started singing 'The Banks' back at them. And being Cork supporters, in fairness, they applauded. Brilliant.

It took us an hour to get to the Anner, where we were

based, because everyone wanted a chat. It was a carnival largely, I think, because the game had been so good. People didn't want to go home after it.

On the bus back to Waterford Billy Costine, the driver, brought us a different route, back through Tipperary. We were singing 'Billy's going to Ruby's', the nightclub in Waterford, because he was always so keen to get back home – hundred miles an hour down the hard shoulder, horn blaring – and it was great, the trip back. A couple of cans, Andy Moloney and Eoin Murphy singing songs. A lovely spin.

There was a bit of a stage up on Ballybricken hill to show off the cup, but no major ceremony. Afterwards we were supposed to meet down in the Granville Hotel again, but I got separated and all of a sudden I was on my own. With the cup.

Half eleven at night, yours truly strolling down on his own with the Munster cup under his arm. I was passing McLoughlin's pub, now Tully's, when the lads outside smoking saw me.

Into McLoughlin's. End of the strolling. I was being lifted up on shoulders, head being bounced off the ceiling while they filled the cup.

After half an hour I got out and headed down to the Granville. We had a drink there and then myself and Tony got back up to Mount Sion with the cup. All the older lads in the club were coming over to get pictures of the cup, chatting away. Perfect.

Every county needs a game like that 2004 Munster final every now and again, something to get the blood pumping and to make lads stand up straight.

It can't all be sterile all the time; that's not the way the game is played. For the county it was great to have that in the memory bank, because for years to come Waterford teams could say, 'They did it that time, we can do it now.'

At the time, though we were delighted with the win, a second Munster title in three years, there was also a sense of 'Let's drive it on'. There were no victory parades, no huge celebrations past the Monday.

That Monday began with a spin for us, however. The city players had driven to Clonmel to meet the western bus, so all our cars were in the Barn Lodge in Clonmel. Kevin Ryan with Justin from Mount Sion brought a few of us up; we collected the cars, and said we'd have one in Ike's and Mike's, between Kilsheelan and Carrick, on the way home.

And it was great. A quiet shandy with nobody else around, a chance to chat away about the game in peace. It was like a bank holiday back in Waterford, but we were grand and relaxed before we headed back. Into Nicky's and the bedlam kicked off all over again.

In the run-up to the All-Ireland semi-final Mullane's suspension was never really an issue. It never became a distraction because it wasn't touch and go whether he might play; there were no hearings we were waiting on. We knew early on he wouldn't appeal it. He felt he'd done the crime, he'd take the time. I'd have been the same.

Nobody pushed him. Should we have? This was the middle of the Celtic Tiger, when there was plenty of money around, and there was talk of people offering to fund this and that for him, to get the best barristers – but he didn't want to do it.

———

Looking back now, part of you would think maybe we should have pushed it. We were probably in much better shape to win an All-Ireland then than when we eventually got to a final, four years later.

But we prepared well. We avoided the circus of 2002, though there was a bit of surprise when Justin went with Iggy O'Regan in goal instead of Stevie Brenner.

We went to Antrim after the Munster final – Justin often liked to do the same thing with a team, and we'd been to Antrim a couple of years earlier. They were flying, Antrim – Liam Watson was going very well for them at that time – and we had a good run-out against them. We thought they'd put it up to Cork when they played them later, but Dinny Cahill, their manager, put down Brian Corcoran and Niall McCarthy in public, and Cork destroyed them.

Anyway, that weekend went well – Mullane led a great sing-song. In the two matches we played everyone saw game time and as a result Justin went with Iggy in goal.

It was a big call. Iggy was only twenty-one – Shane O'Sullivan started as well, and he was nineteen – but they were going well in training. That's why he picked them, but Kilkenny saw that and went for the jugular.

A few things went against us. Again. We were supposed to fly up but the weather was terrible. Flight cancelled.

We ended up on a train to Dublin, which put fellas out a little. We warmed up on a pitch near Home Farm, and that wasn't great either, but we were more ready, mentally, than in 2002, until Kilkenny started with three goals in the first quarter.

When that happens you're always chasing a game.

ONE DAY IN JULY: 2004

It ended 3-12 to 0-18, and we out-hurled them for long stretches, but we needed a goal. Just one. If that had come I think we'd have won, but we couldn't work a decent chance.

We were okay apart from Flynn, who was brilliant that day. He ended up with twelve points. The rest of us probably reached the levels we'd reached earlier in the year against Clare and Tipperary; we needed to reach the level we'd reached against Cork.

A third semi-final defeat, but this one was a real lost opportunity.

Of course, the weather cleared up afterwards, so we got to fly home. On the plane back we were thinking it was a shame it hadn't been finer eight hours earlier. There was a strong sense of 'will we ever make that breakthrough?' too, with another year gone.

We won a third county final in a row, which softened the blow a little. Winning three-in-a-row was a fair achievement, given how good Ballygunner, our main rivals, were at the time. We wanted more – every team does – but six titles in nine years was good going.

We beat Ahane in Munster – a good team, the Morans were playing – and we hammered Kilmaley from Clare in Walsh Park. A Munster final against Toomevara, seven points up with twelve minutes to go, cruising in Thurles . . . and we blew it. We leaked a soft enough goal, they started hitting points, and they beat us by one. I had a free to tie it up late on but I missed it. Gone.

And the club team was beginning to break up then. Brian Greene and a couple of the older lads hung it up: we'd won

135

four county championships in five years, but we'd only won one Munster title, which was disappointing.

The following week, after the Toomevara game, I got a second All-Star award. It wasn't as enjoyable an experience – I got it for midfield, because Curran was the centre-back. It's gas – I'd had three good games in the Munster championship at centre-back and played maybe five minutes, literally, in midfield against Kilkenny in the All-Ireland semi-final. Some five minutes!

In fairness, we got to Cape Town in January 2005. A highlight. I'll probably never go back there again, but I saw it with another thirty lads who were all great friends of mine, which was a great way to see it.

We went to the horseracing there one day, and gambling obviously isn't a big deal in South Africa, because I'd say each of us had more money in our pockets than the bookies, and we weren't millionaires.

One morning we went to Camp's Bay, a trendy beach, to get a stretch of the legs and some nice sea air after a long night. It was a fresh, breezy day, so I strolled down to the water for a swim, not knowing it rolls up from the Antarctic – absolutely freezing – and I came back up fairly quick.

'That's shocking,' I said to Tony. 'You couldn't swim in that.'

(I'd swim in the Guillamene in Tramore all year round, now – I wouldn't be shy of a dip.)

There I was explaining how cold it was to Tony when I felt something warm land on my back: some curry a family on the beach was picnicking on had landed on me. Flew about thirty yards: splat.

Obviously the thing to do was rinse it off in the seawater, but that would have frozen me solid; Tony had to go and get a bottle of water and pour it over me to get the curry off.

Only us. In one of the coolest places in South Africa and there we were disgracing ourselves: me dying sick with a hangover, curry running down my back and Tony laughing his head off at me.

2005 wasn't a great year for us. We played Kilkenny in our first league game and the team was having a night out afterwards, all of us. It was my birthday; I was really looking forward to it until I hit Jimmy Coogan a shoulder in the match. Broken collarbone.

Tadhg O'Sullivan in the hospital said it was broken in half – operation on the Tuesday to insert a pin.

The year didn't improve after that, for me or for the team. I didn't play again until the championship, which didn't help my preparations.

One good thing was Sean Power sending myself and Dawn over to Spain, though. Sean is a travel agent in Waterford and would work with the team on transport and logistics and so on, but he'd also be someone the players would talk to.

He sent us out and I was able to do some physical training in the sun – a real nice touch, which I appreciated.

But the injury knocked me back. I took a long time to get back to full fitness. Niall McCarthy got four points off me in the Munster quarter-final in Thurles. It was the first time my opponent got more than a point off me, which might surprise people who had me down as a loose marker.

I was like a dog after it. We had a right cut off each other in the game – he'd won man of the match in the All-Ireland the previous September, I felt I was on top in the previous Munster final.

Niall was a hardy man to mark. No nonsense, and certainly no chat – he talked a mile a minute and I hadn't a tooth, so we'd have done well to understand each other. I had great respect for him, the way he played (when we got over Cork in 2007, for instance, he rang me up that evening to wish us all the best in the All-Ireland semi-final.)

We ended up getting to play Cork again in the All-Ireland quarter-final that year and we were solid, ahead for most of the game, until Joe Deane flicked back a ball that was going wide and Brian Corcoran drop-hit it for a goal.

It's a year no one mentions, but there was an All-Ireland there to be won. Cork beat Clare in the semi-final and Galway in the final for the All-Ireland. I felt I was back in form by the second Cork game, and Niall didn't score, but that was a bit late.

The year had one fair twist left in it, though.

With the club we were still doing well, despite losing a couple of lads, and despite the players who were left having a lot of miles on the clock, a lot of long, drawn-out seasons.

Padraig Fanning took over as manager and we were playing De La Salle in the semi-final – they were on the way up, with the likes of Mullane, Phelan, Kevin Moran. A young team but aggressive, ambitious. The coming side in the county.

In the game there was plenty of aggro, belting, the usual – they were up for it and having a right go, which they were more than entitled to do.

We were unhappy with the referee all the way through; we felt we were being denied certain frees all day, and when Eoin went through late in the game and got floored on the 13-metre line – no free. It would have been a tap-over, a gimme, to equalise.

The ball came out to the wing and Mullane got it; I shepherded him to the sideline and Mullane went down. Free to De La Salle.

I saw red. Lost the head totally. Ran out to the referee and caught him by the front of the jersey, at the collar.

Gasp from the crowd.

I was frothing at the mouth, almost. I felt he'd robbed us, but there's no excuse for doing that.

Red card. I turned to walk away and Eoin said something to the referee. Another red card, so I had company walking off.

The ground was packed, but there was silence, people were shocked. We were going out the corner of Walsh Park past the sliotar, which was lying on the ground, and Eoin swung his hurley at it – and sent it straight over the bar.

You couldn't do it if you tried a million times. He looked at me and I looked at him, and we couldn't laugh, but it was one of the greatest scores I ever saw.

When we met my father afterwards he couldn't believe it. Nobody could. You couldn't condone it. You couldn't say,

———

'Well, he was robbing us.' Nobody would wear that. It was all over the papers, the radio, the whole lot. When I went up to the county board for a hearing I got suspended for six months.

What could I do but accept it? Some season: broken collar-bone, slow to get into the matches when I recovered, then suspended for half a year.

5

TEARS IN THE RAIN: 2006

Roll on 2006. But it was April before I could play. I trained like mad to keep myself ticking over, and then . . .

When the league rolled around the lads were playing Cork and I said to myself I'd go down to the wall in Mount Sion school to hit the ball for an hour (here's why: when you go away like that with the team for the day but you're not playing, it's all food. Eating the whole day, morning to night, and you'd feel half a stone heavier when you get home.)

Down with me at nine in the morning, hitting the ball off the wall, then back, off the wall, then back and after five minutes I managed to flake myself across my own toes.

Numbness, then pain, then blood spouting up into the air out of my shoe. Ah Jesus: I'd destroyed my toe. It was in pieces.

I ended up hobbling onto the bus with the boys. I couldn't

---

tell them what I'd done because a) they'd never believe me and b) they'd never let me forget it. I was trying to hide the limp as I walked around Páirc Uí Rinn, munching paracetamol. Desperate.

I couldn't train for a week. I made up some excuse to get out of it but the week after that there was a training camp organised for the Curragh, which was something a lot of teams were doing at the time. I'd love that, something different to hurling, building the fitness and good for the morale.

First night, first test: run across a swimming pool with canvas covering. I put my foot on it, bang: toe gone again. Off to Naas Hospital for an X-ray. Broken toe. They whipped off the nail for good measure and I went back out to the lads like a briar.

The following morning the lads were off running at six in the morning, while yours truly was driven in to Naas train station. Sitting around for an hour for a train, then back to Waterford, a sulky head like a big baby all the way home.

Dawn collected me and I'd say she never saw me as bad. Sitting at home, cranky face on me, the texts coming in from the Curragh: 'You'd love this, it's fantastic', 'Some crack, lads hanging on trees'.

I got over it and made it back for the last match of the league but then I broke my thumb playing for the club.

I felt I was getting no luck at all, and hadn't been for a good two seasons, but I had to just get on with it. When I'd break my hand – it happened to me three years in a row, after all – I wouldn't be able to hold a hurley, so I'd concentrate on physical training, plenty of running, to get myself right for the championship game, Tipp in Cork.

It was a year Tipp's Eoin Kelly was flying – he got 2-7 against us off Denis Coffey. Denis was a good player, a tiger in training on Mullane – they often ended up rolling around the ground at training, and it brought Mullane on a ton. But Kelly was unmarkable, almost, that time.

I was marking Redser O'Grady, and we had a right go off each other, but I was rusty enough. I'd missed a lot of hurling. Justin put me out midfield in the second half and I got a couple of points. Dan got a brilliant goal but we were short one or two players and Tipp had too much for us on the day.

We were happy enough to face into the qualifiers, though that might sound strange. We beat Laois, and then faced Galway in a packed Walsh Park. We played some good hurling to beat them, and I felt myself improving, and then we had to play Tipp, again, in the All-Ireland quarter-final.

We were very good that day. All of us were used to Croke Park by then, and we were keen to tick off another box – we hadn't won in Croke Park since 1998.

I was back centre-back and fully fit, Dan was outstanding, getting 1-6, Eoin got a few points – we were flying, we'd peaked at just the right time.

Tipp got a couple of goals late on and we had to hold on, despite doing all the hurling. The win was our first in the 'new' Croke Park, because in 1998 only one stand had been completed; it was our first trip up to the players' lounge in the stadium having won a game.

We were beginning to feel like 2006 was our year. Dan,

Kelly, we were all going well, Brick was well established, we were settled. Cork in the semi-final.

That became as big a game as we ever played, and I think it was the same for a lot of the Cork lads, even though we'd played each other in Munster finals and All-Ireland semi-finals before that.

It was more intense than any game I ever played in, I think. There wasn't an inch. People who think those years were all about free-flowing, high-scoring games should look at that game again, because there was no space, very few chances. A battle between two teams at their peak, two teams who believed they could win the All-Ireland. They were going for three All-Irelands in a row; we'd always believed we had their measure . . .

It was a misty afternoon but the atmosphere was incredible. We were on top, Eoin Kelly got a good flicked goal – but every score was huge, it was so hard to get. Different but enjoyable.

I'd had a good game in the quarter-final and hit a lot of ball, but against Cork that day there was no chance to do that – Niall McCarthy was on top of me every time I got the ball, or other players, but I was enjoying that challenge, all the way through.

Cork brought on a sub with a yellow helmet, a guy I'd never heard of, in the second half. At that point I'd swept up a couple of balls that had gone down the left wing, by the Hogan Stand – they'd run past the players on the wing, I'd pick and deliver.

Then Cork got a free and put it down the line to this player with the yellow helmet, and he lifted it and pointed – an unbelievable score from right out on the wing. That was Cathal Naughton.

Then a couple of minutes later there was a passage of play that still haunts me, to be honest.

The ball went to the other wing, the Cusack side, and I came over to collect it. Because the day was so wet I took that extra fraction of a second to make sure I'd control it, to jab-lift it. Just that extra heartbeat of time to be sure.

Brian Corcoran poked his hurley between my feet and knocked the ball past. Joe Deane picked it and turned, gone. I couldn't get to him and he found Naughton flying through, who buried a great goal.

That was the first time they'd led since the first half, and it was a blow, but we had time to get back. I pointed a free and we got one or two more but I gave away a silly enough free challenging Deane. To this day I don't think it was a foul – obviously – but he got up and put a massive free over the bar to put them two up.

We cut it to one with time running out. Tony went for the ball and was knocked over. Free to us from our own half to tie it up.

It was a dubious enough free, to be fair, but I put it down and said to myself, 'I'll put this over.' I believed that absolutely. In future years I questioned myself but at this point in my career I had no doubt I'd get it.

It was about ninety metres out – at my limit, really, in terms of free-taking – and the ball was wet, but I put the ball on the grass and was thinking, 'This is what you're preparing for all your life, to do this.' The sound in the stadium was incredible – no silence for the taker like rugby – but that wasn't a distraction.

I hit it as well as I could have. I didn't put it as high as I

---

might but that's because I was going for power, and I caught it perfectly, right in the middle of the hurley. I thought it was over until I saw it coming back out the field.

I didn't realise until after the game that Donal Óg Cusack had flicked it back outfield; I thought it had hit the post. I also thought we'd get another chance – Brian Corcoran took a few steps with the ball up in the corner – but we didn't. It was over.

A fourth semi-final defeat. Getting closer, fair enough, but still losing. Whether it's one point or ten it hardly matters.

We gave that game absolutely everything. We were almost too upset to cry. A few weeks beforehand we'd been heading home after beating Tipp, drinking tea and eating muffins, happy; now we were going back absolutely depressed.

It was one of the hardest because we'd done so well all year. Clinton Hennessy had come in the previous year and given us huge stability as a goalkeeper – he could have done nothing about Naughton's finish, but things had been improving.

Cork put so much into that game, by the way. I think it came against them when they lost the final to Kilkenny later. The semi-final probably didn't do Naughton any favours down the line either, because it was always going to be hard to live up to that debut, getting 1-1 against your main rivals of the time.

A few weeks afterwards we went on holidays, myself, Dawn and Ceilin, and it was torture watching the All-Ireland final. As it was nearly every year.

When the dust settled we still felt we could get to an All-

Ireland final. I was 28, a lot of the others were younger – Kelly, Eoin, Mullane. We'd lost four semi-finals and none by more than a goal; two of them by a single point. We felt we were close enough, that we could make the breakthrough.

Winning the county final that year softened the blow again. We beat Ballygunner handily enough, down in Dungarvan and there was a nice moment when Pat, my youngest brother, came on in that game, so he won a medal on the field of play with me, Roy and Eoin. It was Roy's seventh county medal and a sixth for myself and Eoin, and we had a lovely picture with my niece Caoimhe taken after the game.

We didn't know then it was the last one Mount Sion would win. If we had we might have taken a few more photographs.

Toomevara put us out of Munster: they beat us by a point in Nenagh.

What helped us to face 2007 was a team trip before Christmas to New York. We had a great time but we also did a lot of talking about the game and the team, which we hadn't always done on previous trips.

It helped to fire up the enthusiasm for the forthcoming year and to put away the disappointment of the All-Ireland semi-final loss. We still felt we could do it, and fellas wanted to get back and go again.

Of course we still had misadventures in the Big Apple. One of Eoin Kelly's relations over there is a big New York Jets fan – season tickets, the whole thing. He invited a few of us to a game so we headed out to meet him in the stadium car park before kick-off.

'Kelly, where is he?'

'He has a green car.'

Now the Jets play in green and white, so there were green buses, cars, mobile homes, trailers, tents. Green from horizon to horizon, a car park the size of the Phoenix Park.

Freezing cold, raw after a night out, walking rows and rows in this car park past people barbecuing hot dogs and burgers . . . we found him after an hour.

In fairness they treated us like royalty. We had a great day with them 'tailgating', as they call it. Into the game, though, the Jets were getting hammered and we were getting colder and colder – like good Irishmen, we forgot to bring hats, scarves and gloves – so we bailed out at half-time.

6

AN ARRIVAL AND A MEDAL

2007 was Justin's sixth season in charge but there was no
great talk of staleness. No sense that we needed a change.

He seemed to have refocused himself, and as part of that
he gave Gerry Fitz a lot of control, and that helped to give the
sense of a fresh start to the whole thing. Was there a feeling
it was a last hurrah? Maybe.

The league went well – Shane Walsh got the winner against
Tipp, good going for his first year on the team – and we beat
Cork in the semi-final to qualify for the league final against
Kilkenny, nearly ten years after my first league final.

It was no classic: tight, scrappy. Kilkenny squeezed the
space and worked very hard – Henry was just back from his
honeymoon, but he was playing – but they weren't quite at
their absolute peak as a team.

We hung in there. Mullane was quiet but chipped in with
a couple of points and so did Eoin Kelly. Seamus was very
good too – he won a huge ball at one stage and drove Tommy

Walsh out of his way before hitting a point into the Town End. In the final stages of the game we had all the momentum.

It was a breakthrough for us. There are only two national titles you can win every year, and that's one of them, so it felt like a big win for us. When we started it had been thrown at us that we couldn't win a Munster title, and then that we couldn't win a national title, so it was great. It probably felt important to beat our local rivals, too, and to get bragging rights even for a few weeks.

I got the man of the match award, which was good, but it was a crazy enough time for me – Ali was born the week before, so obviously as a new parent I was all over the place.

She was born the night we won the semi-final, so I was getting used to her all that week. Before the match we were in the priests' college in Thurles, as usual, and Murray said to me, 'You look tired.' I got paranoid, thinking, 'Am I tired? I must look exhausted. Maybe I *am* tired.'

I was okay, though, and after we won I took a picture of Ali in the cup at home.

It was a win that gave us a boost for the year, in fact. There might be teams or counties who wouldn't even count a national league title, but it certainly meant something to us historically, as a county. At that stage it was our first national title since 1963, only our third league final all in.

It also stood out to the team. We'd come so close to silverware and missed out over the years that we took huge encouragement from it all that year. That and the training camp in Portugal.

Of all the experiences I had playing hurling, that training camp was one of the best weeks I had in my life. People talk

Me in the early 1980s.

Me and Roy
holding the County
Championship Cup.

The five McGrath kids - me, Pat, Eoin, Lorna and Roy.
I'm holding a hurley even then!

Hurling has been a massive part of my life for as long as I can remember.

Captain of the Under 14s, winning the County Championship in 1992.

Out in the parents' back garden, 1998 - Pat, me, Roy and Eoin.

Dawn and me on our wedding day, 2010.

My sister Lorna on her wedding day in 2016 with our mam and dad.

France 2016 holidays - Me, Ali, Ceilin, Dawn and baby Izzy.

© BRENDAN MORAN/SPORTSFILE

Overcoming a challenge from Alan Browne to score against Limerick in May 1998.

My first ever semi-final for Waterford in 1998.

At the end of the Munster final 2002, after winning against Tipperary.

Celebrating in the dressing room, not caring about my bloody nose!

© RAY MCMANUS/SPORTSFILE

Facing a challenge from Colin Lynch in the All Ireland
semi-final against Clare, 2002.

© MATT BROWNE/SPORTSFILE

Clashing in the air
with Edward O'Brien
and Pat Croke in
Munster semi-final,
2002.

PAT MURPHY/SPORTSFILE

Congratulated by fans after our victory in Munster Championship final 2004.

Lifted by the overjoyed Waterford crowd.
You can see how much the cup means to them!

Springing into action for Mount Sion in the 2004 Munster final.

© PIC CREDIT: BRENDAN MORAN/SPORTSFILE

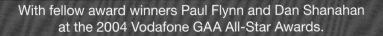

With fellow award winners Paul Flynn and Dan Shanahan
at the 2004 Vodafone GAA All-Star Awards.

Getting past Eoin Kelly in the All Ireland quarter-final, 2006.

© MATT BROWNE/SPORTSFILE

Celebrating after the game with my best Pal Tony Browne.

© DAMIAN EAGERS/SPORTSFILE

My brother Eoin celebrating with myself, my other brothers Pat and Roy, and our niece Caoimhe, after winning the Waterford Championship final for Mount Sion in 2006.

Taking on King
Henry of Kilkenny
in the Division 1
final, 2007.

© MATT BROWNE/SPORTSFILE

© LORRAINE O'SULLIVAN/INPHO

Concentrating
during the All
Ireland quarter-final
replay, 2007.

Waterford manager Justin McCarthy and Cork manager Gerald McCarthy
embrace at the final whistle of the All Ireland quarter-final replay, 2007.

© INPHO/DONALL FARMER

© PAT MURPHY/SPORTSFILE

Challenging Martin Comerford of Kilkenny in All Ireland final, 2008.

© RAY MCMANUS/SPORTSFILE

Ready to face Tipperary in the All Ireland semi-final, 2010.

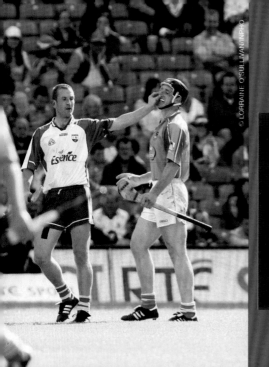

Me and Ollie acting out the famous photo at All-Stars later that year.

Cleaning Ollie Moran's nose in Limerick vs. Waterford All Ireland semi-final, 2007.

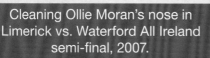

Me and my daughter Ali giving the Munster players a pep talk before the start of the Ken McGrath All-Star Challenge.

about those camps as a waste of time and money sometimes, but not this one.

We stayed in Brown's in Vilamoura, which a lot of soccer teams use – staying in chalets, beautiful playing surface right outside, just across a little bridge was a full gym and swimming pools.

It's all there on your doorstep, so there's no rush. Up for breakfast, get through two training sessions, into the pool for recovery, then shower and head out for the afternoon. Stroll around the harbour, meet up for dinner or a game of golf. Beautiful weather, thirty degrees every day. Great atmosphere. Perfect.

It's hard work, too. The first couple of days you're absolutely wrecked from the training and the heat, and then a kind of second wind kicks in and you drive on again in the training. You'd get a month's training done in the week, and it's good training: no one's rushing from work, no one has to head off and collect kids early.

You're behaving like a professional, you're treated like a professional – there's a schedule for you every day in the chalet. The first session would be running or the gym, normally, the second session would usually be hurling, and a third session would always be hurling.

In the evening you'd have an ice cream, walk the marina, relax . . . every player loved it. We'd won the league final so lads were on a high anyway, and the atmosphere was outstanding. All the lads bought into it, trained hard, and we got the benefits from it. There was a games room in the complex and we'd have a 7UP and a game of pool for the evening.

On the Saturday we trained in the morning and the FA Cup final was on that afternoon, Chelsea and Man United, so Justin left us off but said 'keep it tidy' – that was his signal that you could have a drink but not to go overboard.

You never saw lads get dressed as fast. Off to an Irish bar down in the marina, thirty lads settling in for the game.

It was a good way to finish the week. Everyone had stuck rigidly to the plan, no one stepped out of line – Mullane was late for one training session by accident, I think he'd gone for a rub and when he came in Justin gave him thirty runs to do in the heat.

Mullane was always good to train, and good on punctuality, but we were there to work and Justin made an example of him, and nobody was late again after that.

We came back on a high, but we were on a hiding to nothing in our first game of the championship.

Cork had beaten Clare to come through to meet us, but that was the year of 'Semplegate', the row before the start of their game. Donal Óg Cusack, Diarmuid O'Sullivan and Seán Óg Ó hAilpín were all suspended for our game, so people were saying they hadn't a chance, given they were missing three important players, and the Cork team themselves probably felt they had nothing to lose . . .

And the game was crazy. Goals flying in everywhere. No defending. We got five goals, but we could have been caught at the very end.

Cork wouldn't go away, and their sub, Shane Murphy, hit the bar with the last puck of the game, when a goal would have gotten them a draw, but we got through to a Munster final against Limerick.

It was a different kind of summer for me and my wife. We had a new baby, which gives you a different perspective.

Coming home after training isn't the same when there's a small person you want to see, for instance.

We never felt like we'd lose to Limerick, which is an unusual situation to be in, but we were a seasoned team at that point. We had the experience to draw on, the training camp . . . Dan got three goals, but we didn't pull away from them until the last six or seven minutes.

A lot of people probably remember Mullane carrying a dog off the field halfway through the game, and we were so relaxed that we could laugh at that (it also proved to us that he could mark when he wanted to).

That was the year that Limerick took Tipperary to three games in the Munster semi-final before winning, and I was on Ollie Moran, who'd been very good in those three games. I didn't hit a lot of ball but concentrated on marking Ollie, and he didn't hit a lot of ball either. I had great time for him as a player and knew that it was my job to hold him.

The likes of Ringo Kearney won his first Munster medal that day, and I went over to him at the final whistle to congratulate him, and he was jumping around. You'd be delighted for anyone getting their first; some of us were getting our third, and if it wasn't as exciting as getting the first, it was still pretty special.

We were contented rather than going off our heads. We had good fun that night – we went back to Dungarvan – but we were training again by the Tuesday evening.

Winning the Munster title meant we were up against Cork. Again. They'd been surprised by Tipperary in the qualifiers.

At this point we'd played them in the league proper, the

league semi-final, the Munster championship semi-final and now again in the All-Ireland quarter-final.

We focused on ourselves. Justin gave lads specific jobs related to the players they'd be marking. The likes of Jerry O'Connor and Tom Kenny needed attention, the way they'd run at your defence, but in general it was more about getting ourselves right, clichéd though that sounds. We set up to play our way and sometimes that went against us, but it often worked out perfectly.

We'd won the league, won the Munster title, the summer was running along perfectly – it was probably my favourite year, all things considered, how smoothly everything went. No distractions, everybody was getting on, players in the shape of their lives.

We were dead and buried in that game, though, with time almost up. It was a great contest, end to end stuff, but we were a point down with the clock well in the red zone.

Cork got goals that day – I got caught when I tried to flick a ball clear, Kieran Murphy won it and went through for a goal, and they got a goal from a penalty as well. We were under huge pressure – they had the three lads missing from Semple-gate back in harness – but we kept tipping away. Flynn got a goal and Stephen Molumphy got a very good goal which Cusack saved – the ball went up into the air and Molumphy kept his head to flick it in. But we were still behind in injury time.

That was when Eoin went for it. He got through the Cork cover and had an easy point chance to level it up: thirty metres out, you'd put the ball over the bar blindfolded, but he put his head down and went for goal.

I was back the field screaming at him to put it over the bar, but he had a winner on his mind.

Eoin wasn't known as a goalscorer but he was going for the jugular, which was great in one sense. He hit it well but Cusack saved it; the ball rolled out past Dan who was coming in, ready to bury the rebound – it just passed him at the wrong angle, about a foot away from him.

Flynn wound up and hit it but Sully got his backside in the way and then there was a big scrum on the goal line: I was never as happy to see the referee give a free against Cusack for lying on the ball.

We were steeped to get that free, I think. It was dubious. I thought he was going to give a hop-ball, which is what a referee would give nine times out of ten in that situation. Kelly put it over for the draw. Replay.

I thought it was one of the best games we had with Cork in those years. Stephen Molumphy was a very good introduction for us – he won an All-Star that year – and we were very lucky to get that draw, and happy with it, but it had ramifications down the line.

Instead of having a good run-in to the All-Ireland semifinal, we were out the next week against Cork again for a huge test, which messed up preparations all round. The significance of that goal chance not going in was huge. In retrospect the whole season turned on the angle that ball took as it rolled outfield.

In the replay I picked up Timmy McCarthy, who was a hard man to mark despite a lot of unfair criticism over the years. They led us in the first half, but Dan got two brilliant goals to get us over the line, and Eoin came on again to hit a couple of points (he got an All-Star nomination that year based on performances coming on as a substitute, which was fair going).

We were good all over the field the second day, and once we got the lead after half-time we were relatively comfortable. We never felt they'd catch us.

Gerald McCarthy was with Cork at that time but there was no bitterness, no resentment. A lot of the younger lads hadn't been around when he managed Waterford but for us, we still had great time for him. He never overstepped the line in terms of rivalry or anything; there was huge mutual respect there. I don't know how he and Justin got on, but there was no poison in it. Those games were all about hurling, always.

Without being wise after the event, I felt we were up there to be ambushed by them. Kilkenny had already played their All-Ireland semi-final, beating Wexford – in the curtain-raiser to our quarter-final replay against Cork, which was weird – so they were sitting back waiting for the other finalists.

We had Limerick waiting for us in the other semi-final, who were obviously keen to get revenge for the Munster final. We were on a high after the win, though, positive and upbeat, drinking tea on the train home and saying to each other that this was the year, the year we were going to do it.

The weather was good, and when we trained on the Tuesday in Dungarvan there was a bit of a crowd there to watch us, and I thought we did too much training that week.

I had blisters after Croke Park, for instance. It's a fantastic surface nowadays but back then it could be unforgiving enough, and I couldn't train. Sitting on the sideline I could see the lads were flying, almost going too well, and Justin left them off. It was a mixed match, lads were on a high, a bit of a crowd . . . some players got a bit carried away, I felt, and we put too much into it. I was thinking on the sideline that there was no need for it even as it was going on, given we had a game a few days later.

Thursday's training went fine and we were back in Croke Park that Sunday again. I felt we were leggy; if you look back at the game we were very slow to get going, while Limerick were out of the blocks at a hundred miles an hour. They had goals early on from Donie Ryan and Andrew O'Shaughnessy, and at one stage I looked up at the scoreboard and we were eleven points down. Disbelief.

In fairness, I'd have been the first to say that the scoreboard didn't reflect how well they'd played in the Munster final, but that wasn't an issue in the All-Ireland series. Richie Bennis was over them and he had them well fired up; all week the talk was about Dan, how he was in line for hurler of the year, so they were planning for him. His jersey was ripped off him two or three times that day, and no frees: crazy. We didn't do ourselves any favours but we got none, either.

Kerry and Monaghan had played in a curtain-raiser so Croke Park was jammed, full house, and Limerick responded better. They took charge.

At half-time there were only three or four points in it, but we weren't fluent – we had no period when we were on top for a sustained length of time, which is what you'd usually get a couple of times in a game. We got it back to a point, bit by bit, but then we conceded a penalty which I have issues with still – I didn't foul a Limerick player and Deccie, who was there with me, didn't foul anyone either. Soft, but a huge turning point.

O'Shaughnessy buried it, in fairness, and we got it back to a point again, but in the last couple of minutes Brian Begley fielded the ball on the end line – I was back trying to cover, but he stepped inside me and got another goal.

Look, we conceded five goals in a semi-final. You can't expect to win any game if you leak five goals. That's common sense, but it didn't make it any easier. When Begley got that goal it was the worst feeling, because there were a couple of minutes still left to play. You had to finish the thing. You're not even off the field, but it's over.

What made it worse was the fact that everything had gone well for us all year. From January until that Sunday in August it was a dream year, really – training, games, it was all going our way. Off the field Ali arrived. We were flying, all of us. Perfect.

Then that last goal goes in . . . on the video my head is down after it. You're like a zombie. In a trance. Another year gone.

7

THE END OF THE LINE

After the semi-final there were rumbles about Justin. It was never as blatant as players standing up in the dressing-room and saying, 'We need a change of manager, and that's it.'

You'd read it in the paper, though, that people were doubtful. Or up in the club someone would say, 'Would ye not change?'

We had a lot of respect for Justin, though. He'd brought us three Munster titles and improved us as players. We'd come a long way and we wouldn't have won what we did without him.

On the other hand 2007 was our sixth season together: most of the players had been around all that time and we couldn't get past the All-Ireland semi-final stage. The players who weren't getting a look in weren't happy, naturally enough.

Eoin wasn't playing, and I felt he should have been on the team. Jack Kennedy played in the All-Ireland semi-final but was taken off; he wouldn't have been happy with that. I had that myself later, with Davy, the sense that you're not as involved when you're not a starter.

As a player all you can focus on is that fact, that you're not playing; later you can understand why, maybe, but not when you're dealing with it.

I'd say some of the subs would have wanted Justin to step down. I didn't feel like that but then I was getting my game.

If you take a step back it probably was the best time for him to step down, and if he had then all the trouble in 2008 wouldn't have happened: he wouldn't have had the hurt he undoubtedly felt, and it could have come to a natural-enough end.

It was always up to him, though. In the end we left him off facing into the next season. It was inevitable, having lost those semi-finals, that people would ask questions. But he was there for 2008.

In a funny way what did for Justin, eventually, was doing so well in 2007, because 2008 was nowhere near it.

We somehow made a league semi-final against Tipperary – to this day I don't know how we got the results in the bag to do that – and we lost, on a miserable day up in Nowlan Park.

I was on Ryan O'Dwyer, who'd been a bit of a nuisance the previous year, and I was looking forward to picking him up; I tore lumps out of him and really gave it a lash. I hit a world of ball.

But we weren't great in the second half, particularly in the closing ten minutes. In the dressing-room, then, Justin said we wouldn't train for three weeks.

We disagreed: we felt we needed to work together, that

there was a lot we needed to do ahead of the championship. Between the three-week break and a round of club games it would be a month before we'd train again together, which we were unhappy with.

Maybe Justin felt we needed a break to freshen things up, but if he did he didn't explain that. We'd be falling back in with our clubs for a couple of weeks and because quality varies from club to club, some lads wouldn't be training at the highest level; they'd need another week or so to get back up to speed when we reassembled with Waterford, and we felt that was cutting it very fine for the championship game against Clare.

The one saving grace was the training camp we'd planned – same place, Brown's – so that was held up as the few days that would make all the difference.

We played Cork in a challenge in Mallow on a sunny Sunday evening before that camp. My knee was sore before-hand and it stiffened up over the course of the game, so I came off before the end – worried, because I'd enjoyed the training camp so much the previous year. I wanted the same experience in 2008 to get me up to speed.

I got up the morning after the Cork game and I could barely walk. No training for me on the training camp after all.

We went over on a Monday and came back on the Friday, so it was a bit of a rush. The previous year it had been Monday to Sunday, so immediately there was a difference, the whole thing was more hurried.

The timetable was different, too, with a session at twelve, and fellas felt that cut into lunchtime, which meant they wouldn't be refuelled for the afternoon work ... it wasn't the same. The downside of the experience going well in

2007, of course, was that anything, even five per cent worse, would look bad in comparison.

In 2007 Gerry had a free hand and we benefited, for instance. The next year he wasn't as free in what he was doing, and he was frustrated, too.

The camp was a farce, basically. Players were annoyed. One or two lads slipped out for a drink one night, which would never have happened the previous year, and that cuts into the team spirit, because fellas are thinking, 'I'm doing it all the right way, why are they at that?'

One of the lads was a couple of days late out to the camp with work; another player forgot his passport and couldn't make it out. He was meeting us in Dungarvan but didn't make it; Fermoy and he didn't make it; the hotel in the airport and he didn't make it; the flight and he didn't make it, and that was that.

We had a team meeting, just the players, out on the training camp. We discussed what we needed to be doing to improve things, what we needed to focus on. A lot of teams would do that, so we did it, and we brought a list of points back to Justin – myself and Brick.

He didn't take that well. At all. He wasn't having any of it. We wanted better, more professional training – which we'd been used to under Justin. Why had it changed? I don't know, but it was a million miles off what we wanted. It was stale. When you look back some of the things were petty enough but, for instance, we wanted new sliotars at training, which was what we were always used to, but that wasn't happening. We had high standards, but you need high standards.

Anyway, Justin didn't agree with the points on the list, and we went back to the team with that news. He met with his selectors, and one of them told us to go in and talk to him. That he might pack it in.

We were thinking, 'Thanks a lot for giving us the hard job,' but we went in to see him – like two little schoolboys seeing the headmaster, though Brick and I probably had the best relationship with him. We talked to him and he came around. We pointed out that we were only trying to improve things, and we settled on driving on together.

Looking back, he took it personally. I'm managing Mount Sion now, and we have meetings after games, and if someone is critical of the warm-up or the tactics, say, it's very hard not to take it personally. I understand that.

But he was there a long time, a very experienced manager. He should have realised he had a group of players who'd given him absolutely everything and who wanted what was best for the team, full stop.

We all went out for dinner that evening, the last night. The previous year Sean Power had found a lovely place on the marina and we were there for about three hours, chatting away. A great evening.

In 2008 fellas were hardly talking to each other – a real frostiness to the atmosphere.

A few days after we came back we had an AIB tournament game against Kilkenny in Walsh Park, a tough enough battle; and we won. I'd say Justin felt everything was back on track, but it wasn't. It was papering over the cracks.

The day after I came back I had an operation – Tadhg O'Sullivan out in Ardkeen, whipping out a bit of cartilage from my knee. That put me out of the Clare championship game, the first match I'd missed since starting off in 1996.

I still headed up to training, though, and you could see the sessions weren't as good. Not sharp enough. Fellas taking 20-metre frees in training for no reason. Unfocused.

And that all came out in the championship match up in Limerick, then. It was wrong from start to finish – we went to a hotel for a puck-around and the grass was too high, we were late, players weren't focused . . . that's not all on Justin, either. At that stage the vast majority of us were around long enough to keep our own focus and to prepare properly, but everything was going wrong.

Clare destroyed us in the Gaelic Grounds. Mullane was good, in fairness, but we were overrun almost everywhere. Most people remember that game for Dan coming off and passing Justin when he had the hand out – which Dan himself regretted later, I know. Dan said he felt he deserved a kick in the backside rather than a pat on the back, but it was a visible sign that things weren't going well at all.

I was like a briar myself sitting in the stand. Fit to kill someone. It was bad enough that I didn't get to play, missing my first championship game in over ten years, but then the way the game went . . . we went back to a hotel for some food, and the lads started having a drink and talking.

Jim Dee came in and said, 'We're going now,' and we said, 'We're not going now.'

Then Nicky Cashin came in and said we were leaving, and we said no again. Fellas were talking about what was going on, thrashing it out, and the theme was that if we didn't do something the year would be gone and all the work we'd done would be wasted.

And while we were talking Justin was sitting out on the bus waiting for us, and it surely occurred to him that there were hard words being said inside in the hotel.

The following day we called up to my parents' house, which we'd usually do after a championship game, to chat about the game, and Eoin said it straight out: 'Some of the lads want Justin gone.'

And I said, 'If he goes, I'll go. I'm packing it in. I've enough of this, my head is wrecked. Fellas are doing what they want, the whole thing is arseways . . .' All of that.

But then we all got a text to meet up in the Majestic in Tramore. And as the day wore on I thought more and more about how things had gone stale, how it wasn't as good as the previous year, and how maybe the relationship had just run its natural course, the way things do.

When we had the meeting, then, I heard some of the panellists talk about the lack of respect being shown to them, and when you hear that you realise how bad the interaction is.

Fellas weren't abusive or ranting: they were hurt. Players were putting their lives on hold and when the environment wasn't being run properly they wouldn't stand for it; they'd end up losing yet another year with nothing to show for it.

I knew well myself that our standards weren't anywhere near what they had been, and what they needed to be, and there was a vote on ousting him. I can't remember the exact breakdown, but I voted for him to go. A day or two beforehand I'd told Eoin I'd walk if he went, but the more I thought about it the more I realised it was over.

It was horrible. A desperate time. I hated doing it, but if

---

you're a player you want to do something with the season. I was thirty: Flynner was thirty-three, Tony was probably forty-three at that stage. Every season is a chance, and if you write off a season that early you don't have too many chances left.

Is that selfish? Maybe. If the county board had been more proactive in late 2007 we wouldn't have needed to hold that meeting and cast that vote, but either way it was over.

There was an U21 game during that week in Walsh Park and fellas were in our face at it – taking photographs of us, all of that – and after that we all met up again, out in the Ramada in Waterford city.

Pat Flynn, the chairman, came to meet us and asked if we were sure about what we wanted to do. We said we were and that we were sticking to it. Every player had agreed to stick together and to stand by each other – everyone would stand by the decision of the majority, and everyone did. Nobody did any talking about it or went on a solo run.

The county board contacted Justin, and I'm sure that wasn't a good day for him – I'd say he felt let down and betrayed; I wouldn't be surprised if he despises us to this day.

It was a stressful time for us, too – we were having meetings which went on for hours, and you couldn't get rid of the sensation at times that you were doing something behind people's backs. I remember coming out of the Majestic at half two in the morning at one stage and wondering what the hell was going on.

I've never met Justin or spoken to him since that time. In fairness to the man, he wrote a lovely piece for the programme for my benefit match in 2014, which was a fair thing to do after everything that happened.

I'd love to meet him to say sorry for the way it went, but I can't be sorry for the action we took. It had to be done. I'm sorry for the way it ended; he'd given us so much and he was the biggest influence on my career, after my father, by a mile.

His insistence on hurling, hurling, hurling, all the time in training brought me on hugely, and the same with the other lads. We were often in Walsh Park and the ball would be flying around so fast, you'd know the standard was being raised all the time. It's easy to look back through rose-tinted glasses, but it was terrific at times – the scores we got, the style we were playing with. They were my best years by a mile, I was more consistent and effective than I'd ever been, and the credit for a lot of that goes to Justin.

But it was over, and when it's over, it's gone. Justin recognised that. He resigned.

8

THE NEW GAME: DAVY

When Justin had gone, there was an obvious question: who was going to replace him?

Donal O'Grady's name was mentioned. Nicky English was mentioned. I didn't think Nicky would ever coach against Tipperary, but we chanced him anyway. We contacted him before the end of that week, because the days were slipping away, but he said no.

We trained ourselves for a night or two, and then bang: Davy Fitzgerald was there on the sideline in Walsh Park.

How did that happen? I honestly don't know. One night he was there for training, but I don't know how it happened or how it was organised. Pat Flynn, then chairman of the county board, said to us one evening that Davy was interested: he'd been on *The Sunday Game* and had been asked if he was interested in the Waterford job, and he started laughing, but it was a don't-rule-me-out laugh, not a that's-ridiculous laugh.

We knew from his time with Limerick Institute of Technology that he was a good coach, modern, innovative, and when he was there on the sideline someone suggested – literally – that we talk to him. Flynner and a couple more went over and chatted to him, I didn't, and then he was the manager. He was in, and after years with Justin we had to get used to someone new.

Donal Óg Cusack said it once: when it ends with a manager it's like the end of a marriage, and it is. I'm not sure what the next marriage is like, but when Davy arrived to take his first training session it was like a whirlwind. Big back-room team, the session going one hundred miles an hour, balls zipping around the place.

There was big media interest, and the spotlight was on. Because we'd gotten rid of the manager there was that focus on us, on the new manager – and pressure on us to deliver.

I was training though I was only coming back from that knee operation. I felt I had to train, that I had to show up, even though I probably should have said, 'Look, I'm rehabbing the knee, I'll sit this one out.'

Davy came over to me for a chat, and I chatted away to him, no problem. He asked how the knee was, I said I was getting it right, that I'd be grand – and very early on in our conversations, maybe even that first night, he asked how I'd feel about playing full-back. 'No problem,' I said, 'I'll go in there, I'll solve that.'

I was still playing well, full of confidence. I'd give it a go: it was going to be a fresh challenge for me, too.

Certainly that first summer he was with us he was very professional, everything was set up right – we got proper gear, for instance – and he organised hydration tests, all of that. It might have been a bit gimmicky, some of it, but given we'd been all over the place the previous couple of months, we were delighted with the innovations he was bringing in with him.

We trained hard – and trained well – those few weeks. There was a fair bit of shouting but the sessions were good. First touch, moving fast – it was fresh. We'd been listening to the one voice for all those years, for instance, so that was all new.

Because every player felt he was under the microscope, new management team and so on, the training stepped up. Fellas who had been in the subs realised they had a clean slate and could get a place on the team; older players took the view that they'd show the new manager they could still go.

Peter Queally and Maurice Geary fell in as selectors and were very good; Bertie Sherlock joined the back-room team. The whole thing took off. Some of the sessions were fantastic, actually, and we began to enjoy it again. That whole summer was good. Apart from the very end of it.

We were facing into the qualifiers: Antrim first up, and I went in to full-back, as I'd agreed.

We won and I did okay, but it felt weird. It mightn't seem like a big change if you don't know the game, but there's a world of difference between being able to express yourself at centre-back and having to mind the house at full-back. If you're used to centre-back, which I was, then full-back is a big adjustment.

For instance, we played Offaly in the game after Antrim

and I had to pick up Joe Bergin, who had scored three goals against Limerick in the previous round. I knew I'd have to mind Joe, so I did something I never did before or since: I pulled and dragged him around the place.

He didn't strike a ball – didn't score from play – but I felt bad afterwards. That wasn't me; it wasn't the way I wanted to play. I wanted to hurl away, and I remember thinking that clearly the following morning. I didn't like doing that.

I didn't blackguard him, I just annoyed him for the hour, and that didn't sit well with me at all. At one stage I ended up at left-corner-back minding him and I was never a corner-back (with no disrespect intended to left-corner-backs, some of whom are friends of mine). Corner-backs have to be disciplined, tight – I was mad to go the whole time, to fly out the field; poor Clinton in the goal was hoarse roaring at me, 'Ken, Ken, Ken, stay, stay . . .'

After Offaly it was Wexford, and they gave us enough of it. I picked up Stephen Banville, and he didn't score from play either. Three games at full-back and no score conceded from play, not bad, but I felt that basically I was always a whisker away from getting cleaned.

Kelly was very good that year; he got a rake of scores against Wexford in particular. He was the focal point of the attack for Davy, and he responded well. The upshot of that win against Wexford – tight though it might have been – was another All-Ireland semi-final.

That alone meant we felt justified in what we'd done. We'd gotten to the same stage, at least, that we'd reached with Justin. We might have stabbed the manager in the back, but we also felt the results showed that we'd done the right thing.

———

Davy's intensity drove it, and the county board bought into the whole thing. There was still some money floating around, and they sprang for a training weekend in Doonbeg – though this was before Donald Trump took it over – and it was terrific. The following night we stayed in Dromoland Castle: more luxury.

We had a match amongst ourselves that weekend in Cusack Park in Ennis, though, and it was the end of me being stationed at full-back. I was marking Kelly and I got destroyed. There was space in front of me and I just couldn't get to grips with him at all, with that room in front of us. It was frustrating, and at that point I was nearly considering walking away for good.

I'd been okay against teams from the second division when I was full-back. I could survive. But against the top forwards, being fed by the top midfielders . . . and in fairness to Davy, he recognised that my head was gone if I was going to carry on playing full-back. He said it: 'We can see you're frustrated, you're like a fish out of water there at full-back.'

I had other problems. My knee still wasn't great – I probably got through thirty Difene to survive the training camp in Clare, and if I trained hard one day it was a huge struggle to get through the next session. I survived the training camp, though, and we finished on a bank holiday Monday.

Before we headed home, though, Davy brought us to an adventure centre in north Tipperary – climbing ropes, messing in boats (a lot of what you'd see now on his TV show, *Ireland's Fittest Family*; maybe we were the guinea pigs). But it was a great idea from him – we knocked great crack out of it, the feeling was positive. It was a great finish to a good training weekend.

We were playing Tipperary in the All-Ireland semi-final, and the focus was all on them. They'd beaten Clare in the Munster final and they were building well under Liam Sheedy, another new manager. Everybody was talking about them and how they'd challenge Kilkenny . . . which was perfect for us.

We'd come through the qualifiers, getting used to Davy's approach while he got to know us, the training camp had been brilliant, Davy had had plenty of time to study Tipperary and where we might profit – it was all set up for us.

The week of the Tipperary game, then, I was told I was centre-back. Perfect. And in the game I fielded the first ball that came down, cleared to Mullane, a point. On our way.

We came out of the blocks like a rocket that day – it was back to the days of 2004 or 2007, the way we were going. Seven points up and flying it.

Tipp were too good not to come back, though. They got back on terms with us and we had to drive it on again. Jack Kennedy came on as a sub and put in a huge shift. Kelly was doing well, and we got a goal that was probably typical off-the-cuff stuff – Dan swiped one-handed on a ball first-time in the air, and Kelly was able to get it over the line.

Fair enough, we hung on for the last few minutes. Seamus Callanan had been dangerous for them all through and he got a goal when Deccie, who was very good for us, just lost his footing. Very late in the day they dropped the ball into the square but the whistle went while the ball was in flight – you could hear it – and though they forced a goal, it was disallowed. I was on the line and heard the whistle, and the ref was right: it was a square ball.

Kelly got a late point for us to make it a two-point game, and we held out. Ringo Kearney had the ball and was flying up the field past me with it when the final whistle went. An All-Ireland final, at long last.

We went crazy. Like kids. On the video you can just see lads running around the pitch, like ten-year-olds at Christmas. After all the years, all the defeats, all the stress of that year . . . even Donie MacGiolla Chuda, the RTE cameraman, was shouting and screaming straight up into the sky.

We'd lost so many semi-finals that those five or ten minutes after the final whistle were among the best experiences ever. It was almost a pity there had to be a final after it.

Before that, though, we had a very different train journey home to Waterford. For years we'd been on that train in August looking out the windows, heartbroken, but not in 2008. The carriage was rocking that day. I met Roy and some of the other lads from Mount Sion on the train and to this day they say it's one of the best days out they ever had. The conga line going up and down the aisles was a big highlight.

The players were blissful. Content. Sipping cans but not going that mad, or maybe not quite as mad as you'd think. Davy was cool enough, just taking it all in. There was a sense of 'I told ye'd make it'.

Myself and Brian Phelan walked across the bridge from the train station into town that evening. After all the years of crossing the bridge with your head down, it was fantastic.

Waterford was like New Year's Eve: hopping. It was a great night, and the next morning you couldn't wait to get up. Just to make sure that it was real, that it had happened. That we were in an All-Ireland final.

Obviously a county that hasn't been in an All-Ireland final for years is going to go a little crazy. It's not like Dublin or Kilkenny or Kerry, counties which can expect to book a hotel in Dublin for September pretty regularly.

You have to expect that craziness to take over the county. And you have to embrace it to an extent too, even if you're a player. That's why you play, for those big occasions.

At that point I had the sports shop, and it was nuts. Brilliant, but nuts. And my situation probably showed the challenge of managing the run-in to the All-Ireland final for a lot of us. I had a shop and people were coming to the shop to say hello, to buy a Waterford jersey, and to get it signed. But as a player, was that the best preparation for the biggest game of my life, spending hours and hours talking about the game, standing in a shop?

In retrospect I probably should have taken the week of the final off for the sake of my performance. I took the Friday and the Saturday off but I was drained at that point. I should have taken more time off, because it was non-stop. Stocking, chatting, signing from nine to five, solid. We had one person just in the back room handing out jerseys, all day long, six or seven people working there. It was fantastic.

But that's why we opened the shop at the same time. It was our livelihood, and we wanted Waterford to get to an All-Ireland final so the shop would do well in parallel with that. Be careful what you wish for.

I remember going training on the Tuesday evening before the final, and everyone was on a high.

Did we get things wrong in the lead-up to the final? Of course we did. We were somewhere a Waterford team hadn't been in almost fifty years. It was all unknown territory.

For instance, we had two open sessions, one in Walsh Park and one in Dungarvan.

The first was in Walsh Park and it was great, the stand was packed, everybody excited: we'd spent years reading about other counties' media nights for the All-Ireland, open evenings for the supporters, and we'd always think, 'Those would be great headaches to have, organising all of that.'

So when it came around you had to embrace them. But I thought a second open session was too many. In Dungarvan we had a game in training and it didn't go well, then there was almost a crush afterwards, so many people came along to the open night. Kids were going crazy, the situation was mad . . .

I'm not being wise after the event. I said it to someone at the time that there was no need for two of those evenings, and it was another night for training lost.

(Away from the shop and training I minded myself as best I could. Anyone who knows me will tell you I'm not great at answering the phone at the best of times, so when I'm *trying* to avoid the phone, as I was for those couple of weeks, I might as well have been at the North Pole.)

We trained hard but it was a bit of a circus. And that's the double bind: it's on the radio all the time. You go for a coffee and the people serving the coffee are wishing you the best. The people at the next table the same. That's great, because they're entitled to look forward to it and they're all part of it, but that's tricky to manage.

Give Davy his due, he brought us to Carlingford to get us out of it but the game we had up there was poor. I was marking Stephen Molumphy, who was supposed to be playing centre-forward, but he spent his time back down the field, in our half, and I didn't like the look of that as a tactic; I felt if we took that approach, Kilkenny would destroy us.

It was a good weekend, but I felt we needed more hurling in training, more work. We were up against a team who had it down to a T in terms of their All-Ireland routine – a bit like us in Mount Sion when we were going well in the county championship. If you play in enough of those games, then despite all the polite noises you make about the challenge and the opposition, you're no more nervous than you would be playing a challenge game. You know what you're doing on the Thursday night, the night before the game, what you'll eat that morning, where you'll walk in the parade . . . having that in your memory bank is always a help.

We would have seen young teams suffer in county finals because they wouldn't have been familiar with that routine, and that affected us in the All-Ireland final, particularly when you compared our lack of experience to Kilkenny.

Alongside that you had the focus being put on us – as a team, as a county. Obviously there was a romantic element to us getting to the final, and the media were a lot happier paying attention to us, the new blood, than they were to Kilkenny, who'd been there so often.

That allowed Kilkenny to tiptoe away nice and quietly and to prepare themselves with no fuss, while every reporter and cameraman and radio show and photographer in Ireland was walking around Waterford. For those couple of weeks if you didn't see a microphone or a camera when you went down the town you were half shocked.

The juggling act was hard for Davy, too. He was stressing the importance of focusing on the game, but the idea that we'd rough up Kilkenny, somehow, didn't help our preparation. I know some of the players didn't sleep properly the night before the final because that was on their minds: it wasn't their normal game at all.

I don't know how that plan was decided upon, but I remember in the game looking back down the field at Eoin Murphy trying to hit Eddie Brennan. That wasn't Eoin at all – he was a sticky corner-back, a very good defender. That's what he should have been told to focus on.

Up the field Seamus was having a go at Tommy Walsh. Again, Seamus was hard as nails – anyone who ever marked him will tell you that – but throwing his weight around like that wasn't in his game either.

And maybe we had to come up with something to unsettle Kilkenny, but giving those players a bit of nonsense was never going to do that. It had the opposite effect, if anything – clearly they decided, 'We'll put these fellas into their box.'

I wouldn't claim perfect hindsight. My feeling was that we'd prepared well, right up to the throw-in on the day of the final. I felt we were ready.

But the warning signs were there. The quality we had in 2004, say, wasn't there. Looking coldly and analytically at the way the games had gone for us that summer: we'd been hammered by Clare, had beaten Offaly, had just about beaten Wexford, had had a very good start against Tipperary and then hung in there for the closing stages.

We weren't hurling with fluency, or having extended periods in games against good opposition where we were well on top. We were getting by. Flynner was in and out of the team. I was only thirty, but by then I was an old thirty: the injuries I'd had in previous years, and particularly that spring, were beginning to wear away at me. Dan wasn't as good as he'd been in previous years, when he'd been unstoppable.

Kelly was keeping us in games with his free-taking and movement, and Mullane was in form, but after that we were struggling, really. Despite all that I felt ready, though.

The night before the game we stayed out in Ashbourne, and we had a quiz, but it turned into a comedy show. We ended up shouting and laughing. Giddy. Like small children on Christmas Eve: they're all excitement, up early the following day, but they're knackered by eleven o'clock in the morning. That's what we were like.

I couldn't wait, which in hindsight shows the occasion was getting to me. I couldn't wait for the morning, couldn't wait to get up, couldn't wait to get to Croke Park, couldn't wait to get out onto the field again. The energy that burned off looking forward was energy I should have had during the game, and that was like something which happened to you starting off in your career, when you didn't know how to manage the build-up to a game at all.

It was a bit like the Munster final of 1998 for me – as if I hadn't absorbed any of the lessons of the previous ten years but was just like a teenager starting his career again. On the Saturday evening I remember that striking me – that we were all too high, too excited altogether.

On the Sunday morning we were all too giddy still. The day of a big game like that you're trying to get gallons of water into you, and it can be like a night out, your timetable for going to the toilet coincides with someone else's. I was going to the toilet the same time as Jack Kennedy, and we were both laughing at the frequency of our visits to the boys' room.

It wasn't just down to the water we were drinking. We were nervous. It was kicking in. When we got to Croke Park and finally got out onto the field, you could see the nerves because the warm-up was a shambles, pure and simple.

I know it's the laziest cliché of all time to say, 'Ah, I knew that team would lose, sure their warm-up was terrible.' But ours really was that bad. Fellas were missing the ball, dropping their hurleys. We were getting our signals wrong.

Part of that was down to the fact that we just couldn't hear ourselves. We'd played in Munster finals with over fifty thousand people, and we'd had games in Croke Park when there might be seventy thousand in the ground, but the noise on All-Ireland final day is up a notch or two again.

You mightn't think the extra twelve thousand people when Croke Park is full would make that much difference to the volume: I can tell you it does. You couldn't hear the person five yards away.

I took it in. I told myself to enjoy it, because I'd been waiting all my life for that opportunity, but that was the problem for all of us. We'd been waiting all our lives for half three that Sunday afteroon, and we were conscious of it.

After ten minutes the game was over, though. They tore into us and nailed early goals and ended the contest.

Kilkenny were an unbelievable team anyway, but that was also their best performance ever, probably. The man of the match award went to the team because their performance was just so good.

I tried to get into it – I remember giving Henry a bit of a bang at one stage – but they overran us. No space. After those early goals went in, and we knew it was over, then your head is gone, and that's where the mistake of building this up as your life's ambition kicks in, because the sense of failure overwhelms you.

It's hard to describe, the way that can get on top of you. We had a free at one point, scorable, and I remember thinking to myself, 'I'll put this over the bar now and that's something, anyway,' – and I mishit it totally. I remember hearing the gasp from the crowd when I did that, which is an indicator in itself: you should never be paying attention to the crowd.

I couldn't believe it myself, though. How did that happen? And the next free, then, I was saying to myself, 'Don't mishit this, make sure you hit it properly,' – something I probably hadn't thought since I was ten years of age and trying to rise the ball for frees.

(A few years ago I was watching the Super Bowl and the

centre, who snaps the ball back, obviously had a rush of blood with his very first snap, and he fired the ball back over the quarterback's head; I remember thinking, 'I've been there, kid.')

I couldn't wait for the game to be over. In the first half we couldn't get on the ball at all; in the second I just wanted the game to finish.

Things we'd been doing in games all our lives were impossible in the game. We couldn't manage the basics at times. At half-time we were shell-shocked in the dressing room, pure and simple. Looking around at each other, stunned.

Nobody saw that coming. At the break we were fifteen points down, which was an utter shock because we'd always been competitive. Always. Even when we'd lost we hadn't been hammered. A lot of experts said that that display was always likely from Kilkenny, but those views came out after the game; in a league final only the previous year we'd beaten Kilkenny, remember.

I was moved up to centre-forward after the break, but we were rearranging the deckchairs on the *Titanic*. The game was over. We were talking about getting back into it, when we probably should have focused on damage limitation at that stage.

It was the longest thirty-five minutes of my life. The curious thing is that the noise which had affected us when we were out warming up beforehand wasn't an issue any more after half-time: it was as if that just didn't register with us any more.

At the final whistle we stayed out on the field for the presentation of the cup, and you couldn't look people in the eye, frankly. Losing an All-Ireland by twenty-three points does that to you.

Afterwards Brian Cody came into our dressing room and said the game hadn't been a true reflection of our team and of the way we'd been playing for years. We had huge respect for him and for Kilkenny, but all you could feel was embarrassment, pure and simple. Up in the players' lounge you just wanted the ground to swallow you up.

On the bus back to the hotel you didn't know where to look. And when the pedestrians on the streets of Dublin recognised our bus, it was as if they didn't know where to look either. They were practically looking the other way.

Back in the hotel things didn't improve. For some reason the place was understaffed, so the big celebration meal – which was more like a wake, obviously – was a bit of a disaster. People not getting their food, not getting their tables.

The team hotel the night of an All-Ireland is always jammed with people, and everyone was there with the best of intentions, to show some solidarity with you, but it was a nightmare, pure and simple. All you can do is numb the pain with a drink.

The next morning it was no better. Sitting around, embarrassed. You don't want to read the paper or turn on the television in case they're talking about the game. You can't explain what's happened – the biggest day of your career and you can't work out why the disaster occurred.

Fair enough, you see it happen in finals sometimes. A team which may not have the same experience finds it all too much for them, and you end up getting a very one-sided final. But that's with a bit of distance. For us the day after the final we were still trying to process the immediate aftermath, and it wasn't pretty at all.

On the train down we got word that there was a crowd waiting for us back in Waterford. That was the last thing we wanted to hear – any team that loses an All-Ireland final will tell you that the homecoming is the most painful part, probably. But we had to get up on the bus and see the people who'd come out to support us.

It was raining. Of course.

I could barely stand to look at the people and to be fair to them, thousands of them came down. All I wanted to do was say sorry for letting them all down, but what can you say, really? Down the front there were little kids, all of them bawling their eyes out. It was bad enough up to then but that started me crying.

The feeling's horrible. Absolutely. You feel you've let those kids down, your families, your clubs. How are you going to rectify that?

The recession started in Waterford the following day. I've always said that. Everybody had been pinning their hopes on the hurling team brightening things up with an All-Ireland, or even a good display, because outside of that the downturn was beginning to bite around the town in real terms.

But the defeat, the manner of the defeat, the deflation everybody felt as a result – that all came together, if you like, and it made the harshness of what was happening even sharper. I took a day or two off but I rang the shop on the Tuesday to see what the take was, and when I heard the figure I got a shock.

The whole winter was horrible. We went off to the Canaries for a holiday the Saturday after the final to clear our heads and get away from everything. We landed and within about five minutes a gang of lads from Cork recognised me. Couldn't get away from it.

In fairness to them they weren't slagging me, but the last thing you want is any reminder of what's happened.

That game finished me, really. It made me question myself and everything I was doing on the field in a way that had never happened before. Players that I'd have been confident of marking became an issue for me. Frees, fielding the ball, passing – the things I'd been doing for twenty years without a thought suddenly became a struggle for me after that All-Ireland final.

That only stopped, really, in 2010. I came on up in Croke Park as a sub, and straightaway I got a free. I banged it over the bar almost without thinking and said, 'That's grand.' Thirty metres out, no problem.

I ended up getting four points that day, and afterwards it was a huge relief to me. Not only did it mean that I could still do it, but it got rid of all of those doubts and worries I'd had since the 2008 All-Ireland final; when that free went over the bar I got a real sense of 'what have I been worrying about?'

It might sound over-dramatic or over the top but we probably should have gotten counselling after the 2008 final. We probably should have had some means of working through what had happened. It meant so much to us – win or lose

– that a defeat like that was always going to affect players, and if we had our time over we could have managed it better.

The following year wasn't a huge improvement for me, anyway. Early on I pulled a hamstring, for the first time ever, and I couldn't get back to full fitness. When you pass thirty and your hamstrings or your back or whatever starts to let you down, then it's worrying. You begin to think your body is telling you it's time to pack it in.

I played against Limerick but I'd hurt my knee and I was substituted, for the first time ever. Another bad sign.

Coming up to that game I'd been motoring in training. After one mixed match in training Murray said to me, 'You're flying,' and I was. Enjoying it at centre-forward.

But my knee got sore and I shouldn't have played against Limerick. I got injections, strapping, the whole lot, but I was struggling from the start and I wasn't surprised I got substituted. More pain after the 2008 All-Ireland.

I got another operation on the Tuesday. Another cartilage problem. Lying in the bed, though, I noticed how loose the tracksuit was on me. You could make out my bones under the cloth. After the operation my father said I'd lost too much weight, and a couple of people said to me they thought I'd looked gaunt when I was taken off against Limerick.

I got back training with Waterford and worked hard, and by the end of the summer I even got a few minutes of a run-out at the end of our All-Ireland semi-final against Kilkenny, but that's all it was. A disaster of a summer.

I struggled through with the club and we got to another

semi-final, though we lost to Ballygunner. I had another knee operation late in 2009, a fourth visit to the surgeon. And I kept losing weight. In the shop people would notice it, because I'd often have a polo shirt or a sports T-shirt on, and they'd comment on my collar bone standing out. I often felt like asking them to clear out of the shop, but I held my tongue.

In 2010 I was diagnosed with sarcoidosis, a disease which was affecting my lungs. That's why I'd been losing weight. I got an inhaler and I was able to manage it, and it was a relief to finally learn what it was, and that it wasn't more serious.

I was going up to Ger Hartmann, the physio in Limerick, to work on rehabbing my knee, so I was behind in terms of training. That's not to say it's easy up in his surgery: I often felt like jumping off the physio table with the pain, but he's a great man to motivate you as well – I got a lot out of those visits.

I couldn't get a good run of training going, though. I'd have a couple of sessions and then the knee would swell up – I'd have to sit out another couple of sessions. We decided – team management as well – that I'd take a few weeks extra away from training to see if the knee would recover.

In better news that meant we had some free time, so Dawn and I got married in March 2010. Great crack – all the family, all the lads, rocking Faithlegg House – and a great honeymoon. But when I came back, myself and a few other members of the walking wounded were sent up to Hartmann for a fitness test.

This was a proper fitness test – shuttle runs, bleep tests, all of that, no 'you can walk? You're fit'. I was in bits but I knew I was behind. No real panic.

———

When the league game rolled around against Kilkenny, though, I was useless. Miles off the pace. I couldn't run properly – a ball broke away from myself and Noel Hickey at one stage and he beat me to it easily. I couldn't go at all.

We had a challenge game later against Kilkenny and I did better – at midfield – but in the last pre-championship challenge game against Clare in Thurles I was a sub, so I knew I wouldn't be starting.

I knew I was struggling – nobody knew it better – but that was still the first championship game I'd been available for that I hadn't started, and that was very difficult to take. Looking back, they were probably right not to pick me, but I couldn't see that at the time. To me they were all wrong – Davy, the selectors, all of them.

I trained hard and I was enthusiastic around the dressing room – I wouldn't let myself or the team down by being otherwise – but inside I was like a briar. I felt I still had something to give, that I could offer the team an option.

I came on against Clare, though. Thurles. The championship.

And I got a point. With all the build-up and the frustration and the effort I lost the head a bit right there and then. Beat the hurley off the ground, roaring and shouting over at the sideline. What was I saying? I can't remember, but I'm sure it'd only be suitable after the watershed. Even in the dressing room afterwards I was still like a dog – even though we'd won – and Patsy, Padraig Fanning, was telling me to calm down.

The next night at training I was called out to the middle of the field and asked to explain what I'd been at.

'Ah look,' I said, 'I probably went over the top, I'm sorry. It was just the frustration. It won't happen again.'

I felt I was being judged on a perception, specifically the perception that my legs were gone and that my injuries in the past had done for me, rather than how I was going at that specific time in training. I said that later to the management – 'Judge me on how I'm going now, not on the basis of injuries I've had. And if I'm not good enough, grand.'

It was a good, open chat, and they took that on board too, in fairness.

That win over Clare put us in a Munster final against Cork, twelve years after my first. I didn't start but I got on as a blood sub, and hit a few balls. I put the ball into Mullane late in the game and he won the free that we eventually got the equalising goal from.

I was happy enough. That I'd contributed, that I'd been involved. I wanted to help the team and coming off the field I felt I'd done that.

But in training on the Tuesday I was told that the lads wanted to highlight one of the things I'd done in the game: never a good sign.

What they highlighted was a passage of play where I'd picked and hit a ball. That's what I'd been doing my whole life – a point I made in our conversation – but the game was beginning to change even then and I knew I was swimming against the tide.

I'd been playing like that for years. The passage they'd highlighted, I was back around the half-back line when I picked and cleared the ball – getting it out of the danger zone – but the focus was changing. I knew I wouldn't be playing in the replay.

That was the famous match played under lights in Thurles. A

poor game, a wet night, and I wasn't involved in the seventy minutes or most of the extra time.

I remember thinking, 'Have I gone that bad?' We had a few players on the field who weren't going that well, and I eventually got two minutes at the very end. I didn't even touch the ball before the final whistle. We'd won.

It was hard for me to take because the games against Cork were what I loved, that battle. I'd have loved going to war that night, but the team was changing, and I'd done nothing. I have a Munster medal from that night but I felt I contributed nothing to the effort.

Players always say it's about the team and the spirit and every member of the panel, and it is, but it's also about personal pride. Any player who's starting for fifteen years isn't going to be happy to lose that starting spot. If they say differently they're lying. If players can do that, hats off to them, but I couldn't. I couldn't go training for six or seven years without nailing down a starting spot on a team: I'd crack up.

As the lads got the cup it didn't feel the same. I was still in bad humour on the bus home, but I was next to Richie Foley, and he was saying it was fantastic, his first Munster medal and he'd never felt anything like that before.

And that snapped me out of it. I thought, 'Cop to fuck on here.' I hugged him. I was delighted for him and I said so; he was thrilled, his phone was hopping with texts from people congratulating him, and I was there with a big sulky head on me. I had to grow up a bit, there and then.

Back to training to take on Tipperary in the All-Ireland series, and I said I'd give it a good lash. I had a feeling that'd be my last year, and I got myself right. I'd put on a bit of weight because they'd diagnosed the sarcoidosis. We had a training camp in Castlemartyr, and in a mixed match while we were there I got seven or eight points from play. Flying it.

We had another training game on the Tuesday and I did the same – hit points from all angles. I'd been on the B team but after the first half of the game on Tuesday I was switched over to the A team, and kept knocking the scores over.

Obviously I gave the management a headache they hadn't been expecting, and I was thinking, 'I could be in here.' The team wasn't being announced until the Saturday, but the way I was going I felt confident of starting, all the other players were saying the same, there was one spot up for grabs in the forwards . . . and then they picked Brian O'Halloran for the spot.

The night before that game we stayed in Carton House. On the Sunday morning we were confident of our chances. Focused, well trained. In a good place.

Then I got a text from Donna, Dawn's best friend who was working in the shop: *Heard about Ali, if you need anything give me a call.*

What?

I rang Dawn. No answer. She was supposed to be in Dublin with her pals, and we were going to meet up after the game: her parents were minding Ali.

I rang her father, Keith.

'Well, Keith, did something happen to Ali?'

'Ah no, she just got a small nick from a dog. You're grand, talk to you after the game.'

I got through to Dawn. Hysterical. She wasn't in Dublin at all, she was in Cork.

___

191

My parents had been out at my aunt and uncle's house with Ali on the Saturday night, and Ali had gone to say goodbye to the aunt and uncle's dog, Scrappy, a Jack Russell – and he'd snapped at her, catching her near the eye. She was three years old at the time. It was just a complete freak accident, and my Auntie Lorraine and her husband John were devastated.

The staff at the hospital in Ardkeen decided she'd be better off going to Cork University Hospital, and that's where they were on Sunday. Dawn is a very strong person, but she was in a heap – obviously – down in Cork and that upset me.

Tony was having a coffee with me when I got through to Dawn, and he saw how upset I was. We went off to find Sean Power, and he knew about it already: 'Look, we've a car ordered for you for after the game. You can't do anything now; she's going in for surgery. Do you want me to tell Davy?'

I was shaking, but I said, 'No.'

Sean made sense. I felt guilty but Ali was going to be knocked out for a few hours. There was nothing I could do for her until I saw her. Tony and Eoin were very good to me but I was all over the place before the game.

Brian O'Halloran was very fast and a great prospect, but also very young and inexperienced to be making his debut in an All-Ireland semi-final, and they put him in on Paul Curran, a very experienced man for Tipp. And Paul ate him. Brian took a while to recover from that experience, and I thought at the time that even if I wasn't starting, it was unfair to start him. Myself or Seamus, who was also a sub, could have started there instead, because Brian wasn't quite ready for that – your first senior game, an All-Ireland semi-final?

I'd worked hard and felt confident I'd get on. The game went against us, though in hindsight, again, there was an All-Ireland there for the taking. We were the Munster champions but it was as if we were challenging Tipp rather than the other way around.

I suppose I was looking for a bit of redemption, but I needed a bit of luck that day too – when we ran out at the start of the game I pulled my calf muscle.

Your last game for your county, a big crowd, Croke Park – and twang, your muscle pulls. I had to go into the dressing room while the warm-up was going on for an injection, and the doctor said, 'That'll kick in, give it half an hour.'

Limped through the warm-up, and I ended up praying I wouldn't get sent on before half-time. Every now and then a few lads were sent up and down the sideline to warm up, but I had to ignore the shouts from the team management to do that until the injection kicked in.

With quarter of an hour to go Davy called me over and asked if I could take the frees when I went on. I looked at him thinking, 'Are you fucking joking me?' I'd scored 1-87 for Waterford in the championship, a handy chunk of that from frees. I got a run. I hit four points, which at least showed me I could do it (Dan came on and shook Curran up; Eoin came on and slipped a goal).

It was my first game there since the nightmare in 2008 against Kilkenny, a couple of years lost to injury. I felt I went out on my shield, anyway. I'd played and I'd scored. I could hold my head up. At the final whistle myself and Dan had tears in our eyes. We knew it was the end.

―――――――

Brendan Cummins came over to me: 'Will you swap jerseys, Ken?'

'I'll hang on to this one, Brendan.'

Myself and Dan hugged. We knew the two of us wouldn't be out there together again, and we'd been a long time on the road together. We started together, and we finished together.

When I got into the dressing room, though, I had someone else on my mind.

Ali.

I played for her that day, but as soon as I got in the dressing room I told the lads and I left.

I met my parents outside Croke Park and they were upset, I was upset . . . fair dues to Tom Murphy, who's a car dealer in Waterford, he had a car organised and a driver, and we got a garda escort out to the motorway. I'd never met the chap before and I didn't know what I said to him in the three hours' drive to Cork, but he was dead sound.

To see her then in the hospital bed, the size of her . . . it'd break your heart.

They did a great job in Cork. She got twenty-five stitches. Myself and Dawn stayed there that night and the next morning they told us she could head off home.

Down in the hospital gift shop we told her to pick out any teddy or stuffed animal she wanted. She picked out a stuffed dog. Kids, eh?

It's a cliché to say that life outside the game puts things into perspective, but it's a cliché for a reason. It's true. The fact that I'd played my last game for Waterford, or that we'd lost an All-Ireland semi-final – again – hardly made an impression on me.

We took a few days off work to look after her, but she recovered fully. Not a bother. She's bubbly anyway, and she put it behind her straight away. It could have been her eye, but she was lucky.

Because I had a good club championship in 2010 I said I'd give it one more rattle with Waterford the following year. I went back training and had a decent run with no injuries interfering with me. I played midfield against Cork – the logic being, I suppose, that a looser game might suit me there (Dawn wouldn't have agreed – she felt I was put out there to show me up).

I was marking Pa Cronin and he ran me all over Dungarvan in that first half. I was useless. Substituted in the second half, and the sensation I had walking off was that the crowd up in the stands just had pity for me: 'What's he at?', that kind of thing.

And I was thinking that myself: 'What am I at?' We had our medal presentation for the 2010 Munster championship that evening in Dungarvan and when I got out to the car afterwards, I said it to Dawn.

'I'm gone.'

'Would you go away,' she said.

'Nah. I'm gone.'

I went up to the parents' house the next day and I broke down a bit. I knew I would, telling them.

'I'm gone.'

'You are,' said the father.

And we started laughing together.

I knew I couldn't do what I wanted to do. My legs were at me and that made me lose the bit of aggression that I'd had. I knew it was over.

———

But it's still hard to take. That's your whole life from the age of seventeen and then bang: it's gone.

I rang Chick Hennessy, a friend of mine from the club, and we went for a spin. We had two pints out in The Vic in Tramore, and I told him, and he was saying, 'There'll be some shit about this in the morning.'

I rang Davy and told him. I went down to the shop and I couldn't tell them because I'd have started crying, but it started to filter out then, and all the boys started texting me. That's what you'd miss – the friendship and the togetherness, the effort and the work you share.

The years Davy was in charge, they were hard for me – injuries, frustration, not starting. We'd played off the cuff, stylish hurling for years but under Davy we were sterile, structured, and often boring. He learned a lot from his time with us, and given the systems now at play in hurling – not to the betterment of the game, I think – he started that with us.

When Tony retired he said to me that it was like you'd died, all the tributes and the praise you'd get, and it's nice, obviously, when people say nice things about you. I didn't hold on to jerseys or tracksuits over the years – I gave all of those away – but the praise you get from people you respect in the game is a powerful souvenir to have.

But it's a hard transition, to go from being a county player to a former star. You know it's time, you know that if you stay there you'll only be fooling yourself, but that doesn't make it any easier. When you're gone, you're gone for good.

9

THE DOWNTURN AT THE DOOR

In 2007 I was working with Top Oil as a sales rep. I'd been with them three or four years and it was an enjoyable job – good pay, company jeep, company phone, nice people to work with. Justin recommended me for the job – he was the area manager for the Cork–Kerry region.

I was based in Waterford, Charlie Carter handled Kilkenny, so there was a strong GAA influence there. It was a good job, but I had a craving for a change. After the Munster final in 2007 we had a day's training one weekend in Abbeyside, by Dungarvan, a lovely sunny day, and afterwards myself and Dawn hit out for Killarney with the kids. We booked a place for the Sunday and Monday, then back for Waterford training on the Tuesday.

On the Monday we went out to Muckross House and I was saying to Dawn, 'I'd love to try something new. Something different.'

As always, Dawn said, 'Look, whatever you want to do, try it, but you've a nice number there with Top.'

'I'm sick of collecting money from people,' I said. 'I'd like to work for myself.'

With Top Oil, a week every month was spent collecting money, or chasing money. Selling oil or diesel for commercial use – plant hire, haulage – you'd have to go collecting money, and that was getting a little trickier as the economy began to dip a bit.

Because I was playing sports I was obviously interested in gear and boots and so on, so a sports shop seemed an obvious outlet.

I was having my best year with Waterford; and the main sports retailer in Waterford, the big name, had always been Alfie Hale, who had a background in playing soccer. He was there years, was well established, and I felt there was a niche in Waterford for a GAA-based sports shop. Not solely GAA, because you couldn't sustain that as you wouldn't have a full calendar year out of it, but I thought there was definitely room for a venture like that.

'Fair enough,' said Dawn when I laid out my thoughts. 'Away you go and do some research on it.'

I went up to meet Anthony Daly, who had a sports shop up in Ennis, for some advice, and he was straight with me.

'It's dicey enough,' he said. 'You could have a great month, or a poor month, but it's risky. There are days when it doesn't feel like work – a family comes in for helmets, boots and hurleys.'

He'd been in it for about ten years and there was still a business in it that stage.

I also knew Paul Molony, who was over at Adidas Ireland at that time. He gave me a similar picture, saying it was tough for independent sports retailers and that the general drift was towards the multiples, but he also said, 'Look, it's up to yourself, I'm not telling you not to go for it.'

Dawn's grandmother had an old flower shop, and we went up to have a look at that, and decided to convert it. It was in Ballybricken, which is part of the city, a hilly area set back from the river but around five hundred metres from the main shopping area right in the middle of the city.

The rent wasn't too high, Dawn's father had done shop fit-outs . . . it was all helping to make up our minds, so we said we'd go for it.

I'd worked hard for Top Oil – I'd gotten customers and retained customers for them, and in fairness, they were appreciative. When I told them I was thinking of opening the shop they asked if I'd continue to work for them two or three days a week until the shop got up and running, which was a good offer, but I said if I was going to do it I'd go full out.

In October I handed in my notice, and we had six weeks to get the shop open.

It was hectic. We had to fit out a full shop – it had been a flower shop, remember – while we wanted all the space that you'd need for people trying on sports gear.

I then had to source suppliers for the gear. That's tough going for an independent shop owner, because a lot of the big brands just won't come near you when you're starting out, simple as that.

I had one advantage in that I had a deal with Adidas to wear their gear. I had a relationship with Paul, so they agreed to supply me – which stunned some of the other independents. Starting out we had Adidas, O'Neill's and Umbro, Canterbury, so maybe my profile helped a little. But you still had to put the work in to convince them you were worth the risk, worth supplying.

The rush to get the place fixed up for the opening, November 21st, was going on at the same time. It was about a thousand square feet, so it wasn't that small – there was plenty to do to get it sorted.

We had to get staff. Donna, Dawn's best friend, had retail experience and agreed to come in and manage the place. Pat's then girlfriend, now wife, Sinead was studying to be a psychiatric nurse and she came on board. I gave a couple of lads from Mount Sion a start working in the place. It was all coming together.

Then you've got to deck out your shop. It's not just a matter of your own taste and your own likes – you're looking to get stuff in to sell it to people, so you've to be aware of that.

We didn't have Nike, we didn't have Puma, so that was a headache; getting their stock was the bane of my life for two years, frankly, but we made our opening date that winter, and we had a mad run-in to Christmas. It was really busy, but it was great; it didn't feel like work at all a lot of the time. Some kid would come in for a helmet or boots, and the big smile when they'd get those, it was fantastic.

Those six weeks to Christmas were great. People had a few bob, we'd opened at the right time. Looking back, it was easy to get a false sense of the business, because obviously people were buying sports gear for their kids coming into December anyway. Anyone in retail will tell you that January and February are bad, but we were happy with how we were going.

The forward buying took some getting used to, mind. You're

buying two quarters in advance. In January you're buying for the following autumn, so you go to the Airport Hotel in Cork for the Adidas show, for instance and all the new gear they have is for the next soccer season.

That was enjoyable – new jerseys, different boots, all of that – but then you got the books of photos of the gear, and you had to sit down and order. The question, obviously, is how much of each do you get? More size tens than size nines? Adult Man United jerseys or Liverpool ones? What's going to be in demand?

There's a lot of risk buying involved in sports retail because the jerseys change every year. The players all the kids look up to, the likes of Ronaldo and Messi, change their boots nearly every three months, so if you get Messi's new boots you're taking a risk, because he could change them in two months' time and then you're left with his old boots. If you've ever seen a parent try to talk a child into settling for the boots Messi used to wear last year . . . it's not pretty, and the retailer's left with the boots that cost full price when they were being ordered.

You have the order books and you want to buy all the stuff, obviously, but you can't. You can't drop twenty grand on Adidas because you need Canterbury, you need Speedo. There's all that juggling going on.

We got on well with the reps, and a lot of them were very good to us, but you're reliant on the teams and how they're doing. With Canterbury, for instance, if the Irish rugby team's going well then obviously lads like the hoodie or the jersey, but if the opposite is the case you're stuck.

Same with the soccer. You're sitting down with the order book and trying to work out who'll be involved at the sharp end of the Champions League: 'I'll get in more Barcelona training tops and jerseys.' You're trying to read what's happening and who's coming through in the various sports because it affects your buying, and if a team you backed, in the sense that you bought their merchandise in the belief they'd do well, if they go out of the Champions League in the group stages, you're depressed. More depressed than the players themselves, maybe.

The big stores have it easier because obviously they have buyers, people whose job it is to focus on that advance planning full-time, who have bigger budgets. As an independent you're buying, planning, paying staff, working in the shop. It's all on you.

Obviously that's the same for all small businesses. It's never easy. But for a newcomer it was a fair eye-opener. Take the Copa Mundial boots by Adidas: if you buy three pairs of size eights, four size nines, five size tens, you're talking about a couple of grand for one style. You could have fifty styles, so you've a lot of money tied up in stock. It's always a gamble and you have to get used to it. Then you're caught for space, so that affects how much you can buy . . .

Because we didn't have Nike early on, that hurt us. Man United jerseys were Nike, and I remember people coming in asking for those. You'd try to explain the situation but people don't want excuses, and the odd time you'd hear someone say, 'Ah, I told you it was only an oul' GAA shop.' That burned me, because the quality of both shops – in Bally-bricken and later on, in George's Street – were as good as you'd get in any independent sports shop.

But decking out a family with sports gear – that's not hard work. They're chatting away about matches, kid running out the door with a football: great crack.

I remember a few months into it myself and Dawn went out to Dunmore for dinner, looking out over the sea and saying, 'I think we've cracked it, this is flying.' Nice evening, both of us relaxed after a week's work.

People had said we were crazy. Dawn with a good job in the bank, I had a nice job with Top. I felt it was worth the risk, that we didn't know unless we took the chance, and that evening out in Dunmore it certainly felt as though we'd made the right choice.

I wasn't blind, or deaf, to the talk of a recession. There were plenty of people saying we were hitting a recession, and plenty of others saying those people were talking us into a recession, but we just got on with it.

That would have been April 2008, say, and 2008 was very good for us. The Azzurri Waterford jerseys were keeping us going nearly on their own all that year and we were laughing. Flying. Around the time of the All-Ireland we had to take on extra staff, but the week after we lost to Kilkenny it fell off a cliff.

At the end of every day in the shop we'd say, 'What's the Z?' – the final reading from the till. It was a great buzz all that summer, and if I wasn't in the shop they'd ring me with the total, and it seemed to be better every day.

Now it was going out probably just as fast, on new stock, but that came to a full stop after the All-Ireland. The whole place was depressed, and after the distraction of the hurling season, the reality of the recession was beginning to bite.

We got a good run to Christmas again, had our sales in the new year of 2009 before it slackened again heading through January and February. Terrible. Traditionally it starts to pick up again on St Patrick's Day or so, but we noticed in 2009 that it took longer for the sales to pick up again; the dry spell stretched later into March, before it started to improve around Easter.

The business didn't reach 2008 levels, though, that summer, so we decided to shake things up. To move premises.

Ballybricken was a good place to start, but I'd always wanted to move into the middle of the town. We had a bit more experience and the logic was simple: if we were going to fail, why not fail in the city centre rather than halfway out of town?

The recession was a hard reality for us then, maybe to an extent that people in other places wouldn't realise. Waterford was always an industrial, blue-collar town, with big factories keeping people in jobs; keeping a lot of our customers, young lads living locally, in jobs. When those factories started to shut down and they and their fathers lost their jobs, it hit every business in the town.

At times the place was like a ghost town. Deserted. Empty shops, boarded-up units. We'd head to Cork or Dublin the odd time and the downturn didn't seem half as bad; they were having the kind of recession you could get behind compared to what was happening in Waterford. At home it was bleak.

I'd have been in the habit of dropping down the town and having a scout around, seeing if there was anything to let – and one day I found a shop to let in George's Street, just off John Roberts Square. Right in the middle of town.

The rent was twice as high as what we were paying in Ballybricken, and the rates were double as well. That raised the target for every week for us, but we said we'd have a look at it. Dawn's father came with us and he liked the look of it too.

Darragh O'Sullivan, Shane O'Sullivan's brother, was our accountant, and he was very good. Typical of the GAA: we spent years taking lumps out of each other in Ballygunner–Mount Sion games, but he was a huge help to us in the business.

He came up with the target we had to hit every week to pay off everyone and everything in order to come out with a profit – in Ballybricken that was seven grand per week. Not that easy, but that's the challenge for every business.

With George's Street it was higher, obviously. We sat down with Darragh and he had it worked out perfectly – the electricity would cost this much, all of that. And we'd have it out. I'd be saying, 'No, the margin is this,' and he'd be saying, 'No, it's that,' and I'd be telling Dawn he was wrong, and she'd point out that he only had years in college studying accountancy, of course he was wrong . . .

We said we'd go for it.

At that point any savings we had were long gone. The initial fit-out and merchandise for Ballybricken hadn't been paid for by a loan – they came out of our savings, whatever we had.

When we said we'd have a go and move, our figures were still strong. We did the premises up to a very high standard, and tried some different things – for instance, we had a stretch of AstroTurf so people could try out runners and football boots properly, little touches like that.

We had it open for November 2009 and we went well up to that Christmas – and the following year as well. Waterford won the Munster final in 2010, remember, and that gave everything a bit of a boost.

We'd gotten Puma after six months in Ballybricken, and by the time we got down town we had Nike, so we had all the brands, and that enabled us to offer a wider range to people. That helped the confidence – we'd be at the trade meetings and some of the other independents said straight out that they were envious of what we'd done and the brands we'd gotten into the shop in only a couple of years.

After the buzz around the Munster final win died down, though, 2010 got tougher and tougher. We were at a point then when people were saying the recession couldn't last forever. That was the straw we were clutching.

The figures for 2010 weren't as good as 2008, but we were thinking then that 2008 had just been exceptional, with the All-Ireland final and so on; that things would level out.

Even the weather seemed to be against us by then – that was the year of the heavy snowfall. I went away with the lads for a weekend and when I got home I rang the shop and asked what the take was. I couldn't believe it was so low, but the snow was so heavy people literally couldn't walk around Waterford, which is all hills and steep climbs anyway.

For three or four days people were more or less housebound; that was three or four days' takings gone, takings that nobody could get back. The day after I came back I was trying to bring a pallet of our shop bags to the shop and I couldn't because of the ice. More frustration.

That Christmas the takings were probably only half what they'd been the previous Christmas and we knew we were in trouble. Early in 2011, though, our figures fell off the cliff again, only this time they were already on the floor.

That year was a disaster. We were living on the overdraft then – paying off what we could, trying to get stock in – and it was getting worse. After a spike in sales around Christmas, January and February would be terrible again, and at that stage it wasn't even a cycle any more, it was just never-ending.

The stress really kicked in then. I'd ring Dawn up in the bank and ask what was in this account to pay that, trying to make sure things were covered.

After a certain point I wasn't paying myself, which is something that sole traders all over Ireland will understand. You have to pay off everything and everybody else before you pull a wage out of the business, and at the end of the day that often wasn't there.

I remember telling my parents that one day and they didn't understand it. I told them, 'If it's not there I can't pay myself, can I?'

It was beginning to wear at us. Every day was a mixture of struggle and uncertainty. You have a good day or a good week and you think, 'We're grand'. Then another factory would close in Waterford, and you're thinking, 'Here we go again'.

That took a lot of getting used to, the way things going on outside the shop – things you could have no control over – would influence sales.

If Waterford weren't going well you'd be aware of that, the potential to hit your sales. I remember sitting at home in the evening watching the Champions League on the television and thinking, 'This fucker Ronaldo better get a goal or two, I've a box of his boots to sell down in the shop.'

Or I'd be in Mount Sion training and I'd be looking at the lads' boots and thinking, 'Where did he get those?' And the odd time I'd even ask them – 'Where'd you buy those? – and your man would panic a bit, 'Ah I got them online.' That was wrong of me, to put them on the spot like that, but the paranoia was seeping in.

You end up walking the streets and you're not even looking at people's faces any more: you're looking at their runners or their tracksuits, and you know then the paranoia has really gripped you.

Other problems were in plain sight. One of the biggest Lifestyle Sports shops outside of Dublin opened up in Waterford about fifty yards down the road from us. They'd been in a small store in town but they took over a flagship store near us.

Sports Savers came to Waterford. Champion Sports opened up. With those, Elverys, Alfie Hale, Shaws, Foot Locker: suddenly you had six sports shops not only in a tiny city, but in a tiny area within that tiny city. It would have been tough for any independent.

If we'd opened up a few years before that, we might have had a better shot, but you couldn't compete with the multiples: they could put up a new Man United or Barcelona jersey – and offer a second one half-price with it.

We couldn't compete with that in a million years. The fact that they were offering those kinds of deals probably shows the pressure they were under, in turn, but they had the resources to see out the hard times.

By contrast, going to those trade shows was becoming more and more depressing. People you'd been meeting for the last few years weren't at those meetings any more.

'Where's such-and-such?'

'Ah, they finished up. Gone.'

And you were left thinking, 'Is that what's ahead of all of us?' Doom and gloom.

What was very hard was not taking a wage out of the business. The two young lads would be paid and they'd be talking about heading out for the night, or maybe planning a trip to Old Trafford, and I'd be thinking, 'Old Trafford . . .?'

One of those months in 2011 we'd have met up with Darragh, and he'd have said to soldier on, that there was something there. We felt the same. We didn't owe a fortune to anyone; we were up to date with most of the suppliers – if we weren't we wouldn't have been getting stock anyway.

I said, 'We'll go big for the summer.' We felt we had to get people in, so we bought in plenty of stock to try and kick-start the whole thing again.

Washout. The summer was a disaster – the weather was bad – and we were caught for the full price of the stock. You have to move it on, but if nobody's buying, you're caught. We had a couple of decent days with the Spraoi, the big festival every summer in Waterford, because there were plenty of people around, but after that we sat down, myself and Dawn, and we said it out loud: we'd have to get out.

We knew it was coming, obviously. We'd given it a right lash for the previous three months but there was no sign of an upturn coming.

We weren't to know that the recession wouldn't ease up for another three years at least; if there had been some sign of a recovery, some optimism about a few months down the track, we might have found money somewhere to keep hanging in there, but I couldn't see a turn coming, and as it happened, it was probably 2014 before things improved in Waterford.

From January on we'd have known it was on the cards, this kind of conversation. It was one of the hardest decisions you can make, to put an end to your business. Looking back now, did we diversify too much? You could make that argument. We might have stayed focused on the GAA angle, maybe, instead of getting into everything, but we had had that experience of people thinking it was just a GAA shop. Hindsight is perfect, though.

You have to sell off the stock. That's all there and you've to shift it, but it's stock that cost full price and you're selling it at half, or one-third of the price.

So you put 'Closing Down Sale' in the windows to do that. People see those signs and they stop and look in through the window, and the embarrassment is massive. They're looking in at you and you've failed. It's head-wrecking because you've failed, and there's no avoiding that. You've been embarrassed in the All-Ireland final, and then you've failed in the business.

The last day Donna was crying, she was so upset. Steven Wilmot – Scratchy – was working there but he went back to college and he's training to be a teacher now. When we closed it up that day, we had everything boxed up or taken down off the wall and we all headed up to Geoff's for dinner.

I didn't down walk that street for months afterwards.

Ali was about four at that time and she'd loved coming into the shop – caused chaos on arrival, kicking the ball around in there – and for a year afterwards she'd ask, 'What happened to the shop, Dad, did nobody go in?'

Lads would drop in on a Saturday and chat. Run down to T and H's for a sandwich and run back, and it wasn't like work at all. Having the chat with the lads, and people always waiting for you. That was one drawback.

I'd take Wednesdays off, because Dawn took it off, so we'd try and do something together, but when I'd ring up, the takings would never be that good on Wednesday because a lot of the people would come in, see I wasn't there and say, 'Ah, I'll wait for Ken.' And fair play to them, they wanted to show some support.

I'd given up a good job to try it, we'd pumped every penny we had into it, and we were left with nothing but Dawn's wage coming into the house.

Because I'd been self-employed I didn't get a cent from social welfare, which I found completely crazy. I'd employed three people – sometimes as many as five – for a few years and yet when I went into the social welfare office I was told I could get EU29 a week.

Where's the incentive there to go and do anything? We'd paid rent, paid our rates, paid wages to five people – contributed something to the economy – and then at the end you're told you don't get anything?

What do you do?

The good days were good but the bad days were desperate.

211

Stress. Worry. You don't have a button. From having a decent living to basically being penniless.

I still think we were unlucky. We went in too late and nobody saw the recession coming. I'd be proud of the two shops, the standard of the premises was outstanding, but we had to get out. We lost everything we had, really, but it could have been worse.

The suppliers, particularly the Irish suppliers, were very good to us. You'd hear different stories about different companies, but we tried to be fair and I didn't come out of that with a penny. We tried to be honest and to do it right and it didn't work.

There were people who probably felt they knew all along it wouldn't work out, that retail was so hard, and maybe there were people who took a bit of pleasure in seeing the shop go under, but I can't do anything about that. We had our go and tried our best.

That year, 2011, wouldn't be my favourite. Worrying about the shop, legs acting up and retiring from Waterford . . . it wouldn't be my most memorable year.

Disposable income disappeared in Waterford at that time. As I've said, people might have imagined that was dropping in Cork and Dublin, and maybe to them it was, but in Waterford it vanished. And sports goods are a luxury item, really.

At first it looked like things might turn my way even as the shop went, though.

A new hurling centre of excellence was being built out in Carriganore, on the outskirts of Waterford, and I was asked to go to a meeting in Waterford Institute of Technology. I was asked if I'd be interested in coming on board: I'd have to go back to college for three or four years but I could work in the centre of excellence while I was studying, then there'd be a job . . .

I was thinking, 'This is too good to be true.' Back into hurling?

The only problem was you had to be out of work for a year to qualify for a back-to-education grant and without that it wouldn't be financially possible. You couldn't survive otherwise.

Straightaway, then, my hands were tied: to get into the centre of excellence, I couldn't take a job. I couldn't take a job so I was stuck on EU29 from the social welfare.

I was offered a job, delivering water, and I turned that down because I thought the job in Carriganore was a better opportunity. Knuckled down and applied to college for the year. Grand.

Then I noticed that things weren't working out in Carriganore. The gym wasn't developed. The work wasn't progressing out there. I'd do a day or two a week there the odd time and it was obvious that it wasn't developing the way it was supposed to. Before I went back to college that September the building work had stopped and there were no teams coming there for testing, which had been the selling point originally.

It had been described to me as a top of the range, state of the art testing facility for teams, but it hadn't been finished and there were no teams coming in to be tested.

I asked for a meeting with the lads in charge and asked if there was a job guaranteed after four years in college. At that stage I was thirty-three and would be coming out of college at thirty-seven. I needed guarantees.

They said they couldn't, that nobody could be guaranteed anything.

That was August 2012. I'd wasted a year not working; I'd been collecting kids from school, sitting around, which I hated. I'd always had a job. And now I'd been a year doing nothing.

I let them have it, pointing out I'd wasted a year on promises about a shambles, and I left.

The centre is only being finished now, as I write, in 2016.

We put it behind us. What else are you going to do? It was better to put it away in the end. It was an ease to me, and it was an ease to Dawn not to have me on the phone to her asking about this credit transfer or that cheque while she had twenty customers in front of her.

Low points? There were plenty. Putting your mortgage payments on interest-only because you can't afford to make the full payments. We'd always been on top of everything and paid all our debts as we went, but if you don't have it, then you can't pay it.

For months on end this was the routine I had. Sitting outside the Mercy to collect Ali from school, then back down again at four o'clock for Ceilin, then back to collect Dawn from her job in the Permanent TSB in the Hyper. Months of that and it nearly drove me mental. Up and down Gracedieu collecting them, with the prospect of college which might or might not materialise, in the distance.

I know it could have been worse. None of us were sick. We had good days in it. My own view was simple: you'll survive. I'd seen it with my own parents with the glass; it was tough for us then and we appreciated it when everything turned around.

It happened to bigger companies and richer people than us: the richest man in Ireland went bankrupt, remember.

For one absolute low point, though, there was a winter's evening in Carriganore. The lads working out there – the likes of Brendan Ray and Michael Evans, the manager – were dead sound, great to work with, but I was only working the odd day or two. People were delighted for me but it was so uncertain . . .

One Friday evening, though, I was out there and I was down to lock up the premises that evening. As it happens, the Waterford hurlers were training the same evening, and I was waiting on them to turn out the lights, lock the doors and so on.

After they finished I had to wait, obviously, to lock up. But I'd cycled out from home, and I didn't want them to see me on a bicycle, so I had to wait until they were all gone out of the car park. There are always a few lads who want to hang around after and chat away in the car park after training, and there were that night: I'd done it myself often enough. But this evening I was sitting around waiting, cursing, and wondering if the lads nattering on would ever clear off.

Eventually they drove off. I was able to hop up on my bike and pedal off into the darkness, and as I rolled up the hill I had a flash of 'Where did this go wrong, here I am cycling around in the dark'.

I got home and said it to Dawn, and she nearly killed me: don't ever do that again.

I started applying for jobs immediately after that meeting in Carriganore, and got an interview with Crossell, a merchandising agency. It was the Friday before the 2012 All-Ireland and the girl interviewing me was from Galway. (My first interview for years.)

As I headed out the door after it I felt I'd done well, and the girl asked me who'd win on Sunday.

'Galway,' I said (what else?) and a week later I had the job.

It was the start of us getting back on our feet. Between the shop and waiting on college it was the guts of two years since I'd earned a full wage.

Kellogg's was fine but it wasn't a job I'd have stayed in for years. I was merchandising for them, out on the road, and it was tough enough on my knees: it's a young man's job, really. I noticed there were plenty of other lads working in that line who'd been in a similar situation to me – they'd had a business and they'd gone under.

But the first pay cheque I handed over to Dawn, though, no questions asked.

I'd worked in pharmaceuticals before and I applied to work in GlaxoSmithKline in Dungarvan; they took me on in summer 2013. (The hurling intervened again, of course; I'd been asked to give a training session up in Ballycastle in Antrim, and I had to tell HR in GSK, 'Look, I've a commitment up in Antrim, I can't actually start for a day or two . . .')

But they were very good to me. Back working. Back on track. What could possibly go wrong?

10

SAWED OPEN

To go back to the very start it was Ceilin's fifteenth birthday, December 1st 2013.

Fifteen years old, what did she want to do? What any fifteen-year-old would want, to head for the biggest shopping centre in the country, what else? Fair enough. Family outing to Dublin on the cards, then.

I was a selector on the Mount Sion under 21 team on the Saturday and we lost the game, but afterwards there was a 21st birthday party in the club so I stayed on for a couple of drinks. Three or four pints, no more than that, but I didn't feel great and went home around half eleven.

When I woke up the following morning I felt off. Sick. I had a headache which got worse as the morning went on, a good deal worse than you'd expect after three or four pints.

I said to Dawn that I had a headache and of course she diagnosed a hangover – 'You had a couple more than three or four if you've a headache, or else you're getting on.' I was

---

laughing, pleading no more than four, she was laughing. The usual crack.

Although my head was sore I was still able to drive and we headed up the motorway to Dublin, all ready to invade Dundrum, but on the way up things got worse. I realised I couldn't see Dawn in the passenger seat to my left: I had no peripheral vision. Everything to my left was blurred.

I ended up asking her if she could see me as she looked straight ahead – stupid question – and she was telling me to cop myself on. I drove on until we stopped in the shops in Kildare Village: it was mobbed, the month before Christmas, but I didn't feel myself at all. When we got to Dublin, we divided into the usual teams, Ceilin and Dawn hitting the shops, and me and Ali heading for the cinema.

The two of us collected the usual barrel of popcorn and settled in our seats, but instead of the traditional feast as soon as the trailers rolled, I felt worse and worse: freezing, then sweating, then freezing.

I'd always wolf down half of the popcorn, if not more, but not this time. We left the cinema and carried on up to the hotel – Jurys in Christchurch – and I had to force down some dinner. Afterwards I felt terrible altogether; Dawn was saying to enjoy the weekend, but that night I sweated like a horse. Soaked the sheets through.

When I was still complaining the next morning the rest of them said I was suffering from man flu, but I was seriously unwell when we got to Dundrum. I went into a chemist for some Nurofen Cold and Flu, thinking that'd sort me out, but there was no improvement. Time seemed to fly by: it seemed as though an hour passed in a couple of seconds, and while the girls passed me up and down the centre – in their shopping frenzy – I wasn't with it at all. I felt so tired I could barely get up from the bench I was sitting on when it was time to go.

A couple of days later I still didn't feel right; I didn't see my usual GP, I saw an on-call GP, and when I explained how I'd been feeling she sent me to Waterford Regional Hospital immediately.

They tested my eyes for the blurred vision, but I said that I didn't think that was the main problem as much as a symptom; I felt there was more to it. The hospital suggested sending me for a CT scan but that was scheduled for two weeks later, so we got on with it in the intervening time.

To be honest I'd more or less forgotten about it a couple of days afterwards. I had started at GSK at the time, working twelve-hour shifts, which I'd never done before. I wondered if the headache was part of adjusting to that change in lifestyle, but it was the first decent job I'd had since the shop closed, so I was keen to do well there. We were getting ourselves back on our feet; I was happy enough working there, and the gang there were good to work with.

It was a Friday that I got the CT scan, out in the Whitfield Clinic. That afternoon – straight afterwards – I headed into Superquinn to get my lunch for the night shift, and I had a pasta salad in my hand when the phone rang. The GP's surgery.

They'd rung my mother because that's the number I was registered under in the practice; she'd given them my number. They wanted me to come to the surgery straight away.

I knew well that that wasn't a good sign, when the GP's

secretary tells you to come in to the office straight away. I wasn't long forgetting the pasta salad after that.

My father met me at the GP's office and went in with me. I was fairly nervous and then it started coming back to me – halfway through the CT scan they'd stopped for a couple of seconds and asked me to move a little, which I found strange. Even as they were doing that I was thinking, 'Is this normal, to have a better look at something?' And now after that the call to come in . . . I was thinking, 'Oh-oh, they've found something here.'

When I met my father outside the surgery he was trying to relax me, of course, making jokes, ('Look, they probably found a tumour the size of a sliotar in your head'), but he was nervous as well. Dawn came straight from work and the two of us were fairly on edge going in to see the doctor, while my poor father was sweating out in the car.

The doctor told me immediately that I had had a bleed on my brain and that I'd have to go to Cork University Hospital, but because it was outside business hours on a Friday I was to go home and head up myself on Monday.

He told me that the initial danger had passed, but that it was still a serious situation. Fair enough. I went home but within half an hour I got a phone call from Cork. Come up straight away.

The funny thing is that later I had people telling me they heard I was taken by ambulance to Cork – rushed up there at one hundred miles an hour, in fact – when in reality I drove to Cork myself.

Not just that, I stopped along the way for McDonald's: Dawn had just finished work and was starving, so two Big Macs please. People were surprised later on to hear that this was two weeks after the trip to Dundrum, but I genuinely felt a lot better.

Cork University Hospital is as mad on a Friday evening as you'd expect; plenty of people in attendance, nothing on the television but American *X Factor*, which I hate anyway, never mind being stuck watching it for four hours. Torture.

In the end I got called in, and that was my first time in a wheelchair. Eventually I got used to it, but that first evening I was saying, 'Ah no, no, I'm grand,' but I had to get in and be pushed around the corridors. Overnight stay, and the following morning I was told to go home: there was nothing to worry about. 'It's happened, you're in no immediate danger.'

Furthermore there were no specialists around to speak to until the following Monday, so it was back east to Waterford.

It was a strange weekend because everybody – my mother, my father, my brothers, Dawn's family – was around the house asking what was going on but I didn't know myself. We were stuck waiting until Monday.

That day I was scheduled for an angiogram the following Wednesday: a line inserted in your groin to go up through your body into your brain, with coloured fluid running through to get picked up by a scan. Awkward enough: I wouldn't consider myself squeamish, but getting a line put into my groin wouldn't be top of my wish list either.

You can also feel the fluid streaming around your brain. Screens surround your head and the doctor can see the fluid interact in your brain, showing them what's happened, but you can feel the heat rush through, inside your head, as you're being examined. It takes an hour and I was glad enough when it was done.

I was called back on the Friday and sat down for the news. I was told, 'You've had a brain haemorrhage but it looks as though it destroyed itself; blood vessels can break and that's it, nothing can be done – but nothing should happen.'

They said they'd monitor it and after that . . . Christmas was a normal Christmas, really. The doctor even allowed me to have a couple of drinks over the holiday.

Looking back now, what strikes me is that I had no tests or examinations of my heart, or any other part of my body, during that time. Since then I've learnt how closely the brain and the heart work together, and perhaps something should have been tested then.

To be fair, a trainee nurse preparing me for the angiogram said she thought she heard a heart murmur and wrote me a referral; the senior staff nurse dismissed that with a snigger. I always wanted to thank that trainee but between the jigs and the reels I never learned her name; hopefully she'll read this and realise I appreciated her efforts.

I was off work for a couple of weeks and went to a medical assessor to see when to return. It wasn't the most demanding test ever – putting my finger on my nose, for instance – and I was back in work towards the end of January.

After about a month, though, I noticed my ankles starting to swell. They'd go down again, but one evening, on shift work, they swelled to at least double their size, and blood vessels broke in my legs as well.

I ended up taking photographs of myself in the toilet in GSK at three in the morning, my legs with their broken blood vessels, the swollen ankles. I had no idea what was happening. I was also getting night sweats – I'd wake up in the morning and the sheets would be wringing wet. I didn't know if I was having another brain haemorrhage or not.

GSK operates a clean room environment, so there are boots and special suits to be worn, but my ankles were so swollen on this particular Monday night I couldn't fit into the boots: I couldn't concentrate on what I was doing at all.

I got home around twenty past eight to the usual getting-them-off-to-school chaos, kids giving out about their lunch, all that noise, and Dawn said to go down to Dr Rowe's surgery.

I went down and met Dr Paul O'Hara, who was excellent. He said, 'I'm going to book you in to the MAU in Ardkeen (which is what every person in Waterford calls the hospital) because there's something not right here.'

I went out there on the Thursday.

I was very nervous heading in there. I knew well that something wasn't right. Of course I met up with plenty of people who knew me. 'Well Ken, are you still hurling? Are you still lining out with the club?'

What I didn't realise was that I'd have been going in whether Dr O'Hara had booked me in or not. I have a condition called sarcoidosis which can affect different parts of your body – in my case, the lungs: I've been on an inhaler for the last two or three years and every six months I have a check-up to make sure everything's okay. The previous Friday I'd seen the lung consultant, Dr Mark Rogan, and told him what had happened in terms of the bleed on the brain – the swollen ankles and so on. Unbeknownst to me he'd immediately contacted the MAU to book me in.

That Thursday I was back in Ardkeen – and back in a wheel-chair – and while I was worried I was happy enough that I was going to get to the bottom of it. I had plenty of blood tests and it made sense to me that the brain was completely out of the picture now as a potential problem and that they were looking elsewhere for answers.

On Friday Dawn was there when we had the conference behind the curtain. One of the doctors explained to me that I was going to be put on an aggressive antibiotic, to be taken intravenously every four hours, and as a result I'd have to stay in the hospital: they were going to start me on the anti-biotics right then and there.

The line went in and I was away: first dose.

Obviously you learn a lot about how a hospital works if you spend three months in one, and one of the first lessons I picked up is that the weekend is a disaster, basically. Nothing happens, no decisions are made and no consulta-tions are possible. Tumbleweeds roll through: the hospital's manned by a skeleton staff and it's not a pleasant place to be, because if you don't get your answers on a Friday then you'll be waiting until Monday morning to raise those questions again.

That first weekend was no different: no news until Monday. I wasn't going to panic. I'd be fairly cool at the best of times so my first priority was to get pyjamas. Like every other man in Ireland I've only ever worn a pair of pyjamas in hospital so I had to send Dawn out for some.

'What kind do you want?'

'I don't know. Not old man's pyjamas, anyway.'
In fairness, she brought back a decent selection.

That was the start of the waiting. Waiting, waiting, waiting. They booked me in for a TEE (transoesophageal echocardiogram) test on the Tuesday, where the camera is put down your throat to look at your heart.

It's fairly unpleasant; looking back now it's reassuring that they were focusing on the heart so soon in the process, but at the time I found it fairly hard going. You're meant to be sedated for the procedure – your throat muscles have to be relaxed to let the line down with the camera, and you're given a plastic square to bite down on in order to keep your mouth open for the camera.

I didn't think I was sedated enough, and I have a really bad gag reflex anyway (Exhibit A: on honeymoon in Mauritius Dawn and I went snorkelling one day but I couldn't take the snorkel in my mouth without gagging. I was splashing around on the surface taking breaths every few seconds while the rest of them kept their faces down in the water.

'Weren't the fish beautiful, Ken?'

'Ah they were, yeah,' (and I hadn't seen one of them).

I came close enough to jumping off the table with the sensation of the line going down my throat but we got it done. Of all the things I went through in hospital, that was particularly difficult.

Eventually the doctors came back with an answer: endocarditis, an infection of the heart. They explained that I had a bicuspid valve in my heart: you're meant to have a tricuspid valve in your heart, as ninety-five per cent of the population

---

do, but mine is bicuspid, which meant I only had two flaps in the valve of my heart. When the blood flowed in it stayed in the valve and became congealed, and as a result the heart was more prone to infection.

We couldn't nail down what was responsible specifically for the infection – whether that was an infected tooth or dental work, or something else entirely. They questioned me for another week about possible causes; a few of the foreign doctors asked if I was a drug user, and the Irish doctors explained that I was a sportsman who wouldn't be into that, but they were trying to rule out various possibilities. All part of the investigation.

Within a week or so they'd settled on endocardiosis as the culprit. That made a difference to me – before that I was concerned about what they might find in their inquiries, and it was a relief to finally know what it was.

At least it was until one of the doctors told me that it'd be a massive job to get it right.

The weeks rolled by. In hospital nearly all the visitors will ask you one obvious question: how are you passing your time?

The simple truth is that you get into a routine. Every four hours I'd get the antibiotic – six o'clock, ten o'clock, two in the morning, six in the morning. Being woken up for the dose every time.

I had to get a PICC line in my arm, right in my bicep, which sends the antibiotics straight to your heart. That meant another dose of local anaesthetic to get the PICC line in, but it's better than having the line in your hand, that can be prone to infection. At night, with the line, you'd be half asleep when the nurse would come into the ward with the antibiotic – you'd just roll your arm out, and then it'd take forty minutes for the full dose of antibiotics to roll through.

I took the attitude that I had five or six weeks of this to get through, and I focused on that. Dawn, really, was the one who was left working a full-time job, minding the kids and keeping the show on the road at home.

While she was doing all of that my routine was pretty different. Up and awake at six and have a shower; eat my breakfast; maybe head out and get a newspaper; come back to the ward and have my antibiotics; read a book; have my lunch; antibiotics at two; visitors; tea at five.

You'd lean on the television fairly heavily. My favourites? Every day all of us in the ward would watch *The Chase*.

I was in a ward with another five lads and all the others were thirty or forty years older than me. I was the little go-getter for them, being sent over to get the newspapers, or sweets.

The ward becomes its own world. It could be thirty degrees or ten outside in the real world, but it doesn't matter to you because the ward is separate from all of that. That March was particularly cold and wet and looking out the window at the rain you'd feel, 'I'm in the right place here, in out of the way of that.'

Everyone in the ward had a different illness – a serious illness – because it was the Acute Medical Unit. Quite a few of them were moved upstairs and I never saw them again, which was horrible. You'd be close to a person if you're sleeping and eating in the same room as them for weeks at a time: the monotony is only broken by the odd laugh. One of the patients mixed me up with Dan Shanahan, for instance, which wasn't a good sign for either the patient or myself. Or Dan, come to think of it.

You'd look forward to different things. Having your shower was a highlight; so was having your tea. A match on the television was like a national holiday. Sport TG4 got us through any amount of Sundays – Fitzgibbon Cup games, the Sigerson, National League games in football and hurling. When Cheltenham was on I was the man being sent to place bets for the others: a right Paddy Power.

Having visitors is great when you're in hospital, obviously, but it can also be draining. You're tired because you don't get a proper sleep at night; everybody who comes to see you has the same questions and you're giving them all the same answers, over and over. At times I would draw the curtain around my bed and pretend to be asleep. I wasn't physically capable of maintaining the same conversation over and over again, the antibiotics were very strong and I was losing weight.

In fairness the staff were brilliant – they moved me to a bed with more space because there were so many visitors coming in to see me, but they'd all be gone by nine o'clock.

Luckily for me, my sister Lorna's husband Stephen is a lot more savvy with technology than I am, and he downloaded a lot of movies for me onto a laptop. I got through a fair few of them at night after the visitors went – I followed Jennifer Lawrence through her struggles in *The Hunger Games*, for instance, and I enjoyed *Django Unchained* a lot ('The D is silent.')

The family were out. My mother was there nearly every day: I'd be asleep and wake up and she'd be there watching over me. I'd get a fright to be honest – 'How long are you sitting there?' 'Ah you're grand,' – but an Irish mammy, what can you do?

I wasn't too keen on my own kids coming out. It's a funny one: you're in a ward with a lot of sickness in the air, I wasn't at my best, I just didn't think it was a great place for them to visit. And it was hard to see them, too. In the first week they headed off one evening around half past nine and it was very difficult. For all of us. That was the first time I cried: it was sinking in, that I was stuck in hospital and nobody had a clue what was wrong with me, and seeing their faces as they headed out the door . . . heading back to the bed that evening it was very hard. You'd be down.

In fairness, one of the lads would make a crack then, and everyone would be laughing. That's the funny thing, how the atmosphere is generated by the group in the room.

The days wore on. I read books I'd never read before. Watched Stephen's films. Chatted away to the lads in the ward. But all the time I'd be hoping for news. A diagnosis. Anything to break the routine, such as getting spuds every day for lunch.

The spuds were grand for the first couple of weeks, I devoured them, but after that it got fairly tired. If you had a big roast dinner one day you'd be delighted, but if you got it three, four, five days in a row you wouldn't be long getting bored by it.

(In fairness, Mossy, a pal of mine, sneaked in a snack box one evening. He was after working twelve hours, dropped into KFC for me and brought it over to the hospital: 'Mac, you've some life here, boy.')

It got so bad that for a while the smell of potatoes was making me sick, but on the flip side the tea you'd get in the evening would always be tasty. Chicken breast in breadcrumbs, or a sausage roll. A cup of tea with a couple of biscuits – a couple for most of the lads in the ward, but the nurses were very good to me: six or seven biscuits or an extra dessert for a man with a sweet tooth.

As time passed the doctors began to drop little hints. Suggestions. There might be open-heart surgery involved. Valves were mentioned. I heard 'We'll cross that bridge when we come to it' and variations of that, but obviously they were preparing me for that possibility, dropping it into conversations so that it wouldn't be a shock when it had to be considered.

I was in the crossing-that-bridge-when-we-come-to-it camp myself, but Dawn was keen enough on me having the surgery – 'Get it done and you'll be right, then,' – but I needed a bit of convincing about having my open-heart surgery. In the end the decision wasn't up for discussion, really: we had no choice in the matter.

After five weeks there was a bit of progress. I was allowed to slip off home in between doses of antibiotics, so long as I was back for the next dose. That meant a fair improvement in the food department as much as anything else.

It was still hard to go back out the front door of my own house at nine o'clock, to head back to Ardkeen for the antibiotics, but it was a bit of variety. A change of scenery. A lot of the lads in the ward never got out, so at least I was seeing the outside world before I got back into my pyjamas.

Dr O'Callaghan and Dr Owens were the cardiac specialists and were very good to me. They stressed that it was something that could happen to anyone; they were aware I'd played hurling, that I'd trained hard for years and they were keen to get across that the condition had been there since birth. I'd always had a bicuspid valve in my heart and I'd just been lucky it hadn't come against me when I was playing for Waterford.

When I look back now, though, I wonder if it was a factor in the last few seasons that I played intercounty. I'd train hard for a few weeks and I'd be destroyed. Far more tired than I should have been; in my prime when I was fit, I loved the hardship of a tough training session and I felt great.

Even then I'd be right on the edge in terms of weight – it was easy to get too skinny, to be too light – but those last few years I felt I was too thin and couldn't put on weight, and I wonder if the valve was coming against me then.

When the replacement valve surgery began to get mentioned more and more, then Professor Redmond, who eventually carried it out, came into the reckoning.

A lovely guy, small, charismatic – very confident, which is reassuring to see in someone who'll be saving your life. He chatted away to myself and Dawn one Friday morning about what the surgery entailed, and she was as enthusiastic then about it as ever.

I wasn't as gung-ho about it but gradually it became our only hope, and dates started to get mentioned. One huge advantage I had was that a friend of our family, Cait Morrissey, worked in the cardio rehab department in Ardkeen: she'd help patients with heart problems to prehab and rehab when it came to serious surgery, and she gave me a booklet on the surgery.

'No bother, Cait,' I said and opened the booklet.

Page one: having your chest-bone sawed open.

Page two: during surgery your ribs are clamped open and held apart.

Now, I had plenty of operations during my career – to fix broken fingers, repair ankles and shoulders, all of that. Stitches. Broken teeth. My attitude was always, 'Ah, when I'm under it doesn't really matter.' This was different.

'You have to pay attention to this,' Cait told me. 'If you wake up after this not knowing what to expect, then you'll be in trouble.'

She was brilliant. She explained things and chatted to Dawn about it, what to expect. She helped me to understand how serious the procedure was, how much punishment your body would take.

In the end, though, there was no element of choice involved. It was the only option on the table, and it was going to have to be done. There were plenty of the lads who visited me who'd had heart surgery too, and who could tell me what to expect. And they stressed that for all the hardship of the operation and afterwards, you'd feel the benefit once you recovered.

One of them was Pat Flynn, Paul Flynn's dad. He'd had open-heart surgery a few years beforehand and he told me it was like getting hit by a bus.

'Like the bus down in Cork, Pat?' I asked him.

(Full disclosure: Pat worked in the glass and then fell in with CIE, and he often drove the Waterford team bus. We had a championship game in Cork one summer and we pucked around in St Finbarr's club before heading to Páirc Uí Chaoimh. I asked Pat if I could drive the bus around the car park and he gave me the keys; there I was, the driver's cap on, laughing my head off, zooming around and around an hour before we lined out in front of forty thousand people. Sure I could have turned the bus over and wiped the team out, the way I drive.)

But it was good to talk to him and the others who'd been through it. They were all positive about it, and that was encouraging.

After eight weeks or so of waiting on Professor Redmond's availability, I got the word one Wednesday: I was going up to the Beacon in Dublin the next Monday and I'd be operated on the following morning: April 16th.

That was a hard weekend. Dawn is an Irish dancing teacher and the World Championships of Irish dancing was on that weekend in Killarney. She didn't want to go but I insisted – she's into it, it's her passion, Ali loves it, Ceilin was still dancing at that time, it was something they all went to and enjoyed. The highlight of their year.

I was going up to Dublin by ambulance on the Monday and I told them I'd prefer them to go to Killarney the weekend before. I was getting a bit nervous about the operation and I didn't want to see them upset and worrying all that weekend, particularly if there was something they could go to and enjoy.

Saying goodbye to them that day . . . that was probably the lowest point. It was horrible, the hardest. Ali was bawling: she said, 'I've never seen my dad crying,' which would break your heart to hear.

She's tough enough, she's been through a fair bit herself and I was trying myself not to cry in front of her and the rest of them, but that was very difficult, going out the door that evening.

That Sunday I went up to my parents' house for dinner and my mother says – I don't remember this – that I asked them to bring me back to the hospital and told them not to come out in the morning. My father dropped me back out and I could see he was nervous, so I ran into the hospital from the car, more or less, before he got upset. Or I did.

I was brought to the Beacon by ambulance. All I had heard for the couple of days before that in the hospital was that I'd get sick in the ambulance – you're facing the wrong way, lying down, it's noisy in the ambulance, the sensation makes you vomit, or at least that's what I was told, and that was playing on my mind all that weekend. I didn't sleep Sunday thinking about how I was going to get sick all over the paramedics in the ambulance. Never mind the major surgery the day after the trip.

And it didn't turn out like that at all, of course. The ambulance lads were sound, they let me sit up and we chatted away all the way up to Dublin.

But before we left Waterford . . . we went along the quays to take the motorway up, and it was a beautiful day, a pet day in April with the weather beginning to improve. The river was like a pane of glass, it was so still, and it really struck me because I'd been stuck in for so long and hadn't seen it properly. And it also hit home. That I was leaving Waterford.

In the Beacon I was popped into a wheelchair again but I was beyond being conscious or shy about being seen in a wheelchair at that stage. Before the surgery I was in a room with another chap, and he recognised me from the hurling.

We had a good chat about the season coming down the tracks. Then I got a menu. Hallelujah.

After Ardkeen that was a major boost – I rang Dawn to tell her – and I had a four-course meal. Great stuff.

The staff came to talk to me about the operation then, and I had to sign a waiver. That brought me face to face with the reality. Dawn and Ali landed in from Killarney then, and when they left me that evening it was horrible.

I would have been optimistic, but signing waivers, saying goodbye to the two of them . . . it all begins to sink in on you. Your life is going to be in other people's hands. You're going to be on life support for hours so that you'll survive, pure and simple. I'd had my knee cartilage operated on, and a screw put into my shoulder, but this was serious, serious surgery.

Last thing that night, a nurse gave me shaving cream and a razor – a little Bic, no Gillette Mach3 – and told me to shave my chest. First time I'd ever had to do that. When I went into the bathroom I saw myself in the mirror: gaunt, no muscle anywhere. I looked like a little plucked turkey with all the weight I'd lost.

That was the point I felt really down. Sad. I was thinking to myself, 'Christ, Mac . . .'

I knew there were plenty of people worse off than me, but that was a low point. It was the only time, really, that I felt sorry for myself.

But I slapped on the shaving cream and started with the razor.

Someone had told me that you could get a tablet that would sedate you the night before the operation, and I was fairly keen on getting one, given what I was facing the next morning. I'd been taking a sleeping tablet the odd time in Ardkeen because it's hard to sleep at times in a hospital, there's so much going on; I didn't get one in the Beacon that night, though.

I was desperate to get some rest, and I must have nodded off at some stage, because I remember being woken up at six o'clock and wheeled down. I took off my wedding ring.

The surgeon came out: 'Ready to go?' and then the mask came down over my face with the anaesthetic.

In all the operations I'd had I'd look forward to that, funnily enough, to relaxing just as they put you under. That morning in the Beacon I can't remember if they asked me to count backwards from ten or not; I just went out.

When I came to I was in the Intensive Care Unit. I don't remember my eyes coming open and thinking 'I'm alive!'

I was operated on for seven or eight hours: the aortic valve was replaced, and so was the aortic root.

It's a huge operation, and afterwards you're in and out of it; half-conscious for a couple of days, really. Tubes up your nose, down your throat. A catheter downstairs. Tubes up under your ribs sucking out any fluid or blood out of your lungs. You're awake but you're not really with it. Not right.

I remember the sweat flowing out of me, and not being able to move to wipe myself. You can't move your arms; you can barely lift your head; after all, your chest's been broken open.

All that Wednesday I spent looking at the clock on the wall. Sweating. Sleeping.

Thursday morning they took the tubes out from under my ribs, which was one of the worst sensations I've ever experienced.

It's progress, because getting them out eases the pressure there, but there's no easy way to do it. They just yank them out, and you can feel both of them being wrenched clean out of your body.

But you're made to walk a few steps on the Thursday, just two days after the operation, to get you going. It's like learning to walk again. You're being held up by the arms like a baby, your head is just a dead weight you can't budge, you're trying to move your feet . . . but it's important to move. It gets you started on the recovery.

I was brought back to my room. The pain was kicking in then, and it was rough, because even though you're on serious painkillers, everything hurts.

For instance, it's important to get the phlegm up out of your chest, so you're made to cough. You're coughing and sending that vibration through your chest, which was sawed open the day before: agony. A sneeze and it's like getting hit by a car. The worst belt you ever got.

Everything helps. Everything hurts. You get a little tube and you've to suck on it, to get little tiny balls in it to rise up: that's to open your lungs and get them working properly, which is great, but it's like having a knife dragged down the sides of your chest.

No matter what I did that Thursday night I couldn't get comfortable. Sore, sweating, unable to move, calling the nurses to empty the catheter, which kept filling up – I didn't sleep a wink.

There wasn't any sense of 'I made it, that's great'. The pain, the sickness . . . the amount of drugs you're on, the trauma your body has gone through means your body's in shock, basically, and you're being kept alive by a machine. It's just that you're conscious and you've got to try to recover as well as you can.

Getting the catheter out after a couple of days was another step. More progress. Though it was also pretty uncomfortable. In fairness to Dawn, she said she'd stay and help, but the nurse put the run on her – 'Oh no, no, you've to go' – and that was just pulled out. And out and out. I was thinking, 'Jesus, is this thing ever going to come out?'

There's no dignity in it. I couldn't lift my head off the pillow to look around, let alone wash myself. A nurse did that. I'd have been mortified six months earlier but sure at that stage embarrassment didn't even enter my head.

They were all very good – Dawn, my parents – keeping me company in those few days, even though I was out of it. After a couple of days Eoin came up from Waterford to see me and they were all saying 'Ah, he's looking well, he's improving', but when he saw me he got some shock: he didn't speak for about an hour, just sat there staring.

I improved bit by bit. Once the heart started working properly I started feeling queasy, almost seasick, because it's thumping so hard. I could feel it moving in my chest, hammering away, working hard, but it settled down soon enough.

By then I was on thirty tablets a day. The doctors were worried about infections, so they kept the dosage high while I recovered. The weekend after the operation was actually Ali's birthday, so Dawn brought her and Ceilin to Dundrum Shopping Centre for a treat.

(Ali brought that up recently: 'Remember the year you missed my birthday because you were in the Beacon?' And her mother said, 'The time he was trying to stay alive to mind you, you mean?')

By the following Tuesday I was able to walk down to the shop for the paper. And when I say walk, I mean walk: Rob Heffernan was under no pressure from me, the speed I was going at. But I was mobile. I could watch television without feeling sick, though all there was to watch was Indian Premier League Cricket, which was how I became an expert on cricket; either that or Dom the house man, running around Britain finding dodgy builders, or *A Place In The Sun*. All the daytime television greats.

As I got stronger I was able to stay awake later – the Champions League game between Real Madrid and Bayern Munich was a highlight – and I began to enjoy myself. There was a documentary on one evening about Rolls Royce cars, the Thursday week after the operation, and it hit me: I was happy. I'd made it. I was looking forward to getting home.

The Thursday morning the nurse came into me and said I'd be going back to the hospital in Waterford the next day, and I was delighted. To celebrate I went up to the rooftop restaurant to celebrate: view out over Dublin, menu in front of me. My father rang.

'I'll be heading back down in the morning,' I told him.

'Great,' he said. 'Where are you now?'

'Up in the restaurant. Having a fry.'

And that was my celebration: eggs, rashers, sausages.

From my bedroom in the Beacon I could look out through the window. A tile shop. Two car dealerships. When I was just after the operation I couldn't move my head, and I'd be staring out at them.

———

But when I was able to get up on my feet I could take in the view beyond the tile shop and the cars on the forecourts, and I could see a hurling pitch.

You turn right after the roundabout for the Beacon, and the pitch is on your left. It was May. Sunny. I don't know what club it was but I was looking in at lads training, chatting, pucking around.

And that was great. I was thinking that I couldn't wait to go to a hurling game again, to watch a game live. You'd give out about the game at times and how it takes over your life, but that got the enthusiasm going in me.

Another evening I was able to walk down to a coffee shop in the hospital, and I could see people going jogging, heading out with gear bags, walking, and that encouraged me too. It made me feel like I had my life back.

Those two weeks in the Beacon felt longer than the eight weeks in Ardkeen. People came up to see me – Tony Browne, the Greenes, all my pals – and I appreciated it, but between the operation and the recovery I was glad to head south again.

When I got to Ardkeen the wheelchair was rolled out for me again. A couple of the nurses told me I'd lost some weight since I'd gone to Dublin. They were right.

The Wednesday or Thursday afterwards I was let home for good. Dawn collected me and we pulled in . . . it was an unbelievable feeling to be back. No banners, no posters, but after eleven weeks away, just to be back in your own place. Sit where you liked. Cup of coffee whenever you wanted one. Put whatever you liked on the television. Even the Indian Premier League Cricket.

———

Sleeping was tough for a while. I was very cold a lot of the time, which happens to people when they have heart surgery, and I was under twelve stones in weight. But I was keen to start rehab, and I stuck to the programme I was given.

To give an idea of what that involved, it started off with five minutes of walking every day. Five minutes. The nurse who talked to me about it warned me not to overdo it, but inside I was thinking 'five minutes? Come on . . .'

That first day I headed off out the door. First session. Five minutes? No problem. Down the road and back.

And when I got back I had to go to sleep. I was like someone who'd trained full-on for an hour and a half. The next day, though, I went again. Another five minutes. The day after, the same.

Every week you add another few minutes to the walk, and by the fourth week you're up to a twenty-five minute walk. Getting there. Progress.

That first week, though, I bumped into one of the neighbours on my walk. Because I was feeling cold I'd gone out with a hat, scarf and jacket, though it was May, and I met her on my way back, and she was very encouraging: 'You're looking great, fair play.' Of course, she only told me a couple of months later she got the fright of her life when she saw me.

I wasn't home more than two weeks when the President of Mount Sion, Dickie Roche, passed away. Dickie won fifteen county championships with Mount Sion, I knew him all my life and looked up to him, his grandsons Richie and Stephen are on the team now . . . there was no way I'd miss that funeral.

I was getting dressed to head out to it and Dawn was slagging me: 'You're looking too well altogether, people will think you weren't sick at all.' We were laughing but I was delighted. I felt I was getting better all the time – I was certainly a lot better than I'd been up in the Beacon after the operation.

When I went to the funeral, though, people couldn't believe how gaunt I was. They were all telling me to my face I looked great, but they were ringing my mother and father afterwards to say how thin I was. When we went back to the clubhouse it was as if some fellas wouldn't come over to me; I thought I was improving, and I was, but for people who mightn't have seen me for six months I looked shockingly sick.

I was on antibiotics all this time. The PICC line was still in, and Dawn was shown by a nurse how to administer them – we'd put the antibiotics in the fridge and take them out when we needed them, and I was taking those for a good six weeks after the operation. I was on warfarin and some other drugs as well, so I was still in recovery. I had to have an injection into my stomach every day, for instance, and my stomach got very bruised as a result (Dawn seemed to take a lot of pleasure in giving me those injections, actually).

Obviously having spent years keeping fit with Waterford helped me in terms of my general health facing into that time. The problem sometimes is that I'd be a little too used to pushing myself. After a few weeks of my walking I was out in the gardens in Mount Congreve and I walked a bit too far and got a bit of a fright. I had to sit down and have an ice cream to recover.

After those six weeks I was okay, though. Once I got off those tablets, really, I was set.

The surgeon put in a replacement pig tissue valve because I was so young. I'm active, I like to keep fit, to have a pint, so I got the pig tissue option. There's a mechanical valve option but if you have that then you're on warfarin, and then you're very limited in what you can and can't do.

With the pig tissue valve you don't take medication after the first six weeks, life is normal – I could probably play hurling again if my knees weren't destroyed – but it only lasts ten years. I'll have to have this done again in ten years, but I don't really think about that.

I had to do cardio rehab for six weeks in Ardkeen and I was the youngest in the group by thirty years, I'd say. Cait and Stephen are in charge of it and they're brilliant. You're monitored for the training rate you must stick to in the exercises, five minutes on each machine, everything is measured – it was a great routine, an hour twice a week, a great group and everyone encouraging each other. Hurling talk. Enjoyable.

A lot of people can get very down, very introverted, after heart surgery. It didn't happen to me but it's recognised as a huge part of the recovery, having a good mental outlook.

For me that summer was fantastic once we rolled into June. Eoin had spoken to me about coming in to work with him in the coffee business, so that was waiting in September. The weather was beautiful and I said, 'I'll enjoy these few weeks.' I got a bike and started cycling, and went for a swim nearly every day. In the sun my hair went blond and I got a great tan, I was like a Swede walking around Waterford. Going for walks, getting stronger.

If you like, I went back to my childhood twenty-odd years later. A summer with no responsibilities, just cycling around and taking the sun. Splashing around Tramore and having ice cream on the prom. The schedule I kept as a teenager, just updated to my mid-thirties.

Overall it was a desperately hard time, though. Quite apart from the physical toll, you're worried about your wife, about the kids, about your parents. About your job.

I was working in GSK but I hadn't been there long enough to be made permanent. I'd been self-employed before that. I thought I'd get social welfare when I was off work – but I hadn't enough stamps built up. I was so sick that I couldn't really focus on that; I was just trying to recover. GSK were very good to me, actually, but the system in Ireland wouldn't be very supportive of someone who's been self-employed.

It all fell on Dawn, really. How she managed it, I don't know. Paying a mortgage, keeping the house going, the kids . . . it was a hard, hard time.

I don't think about those days much now, and that time doesn't affect my day-to-day life too much either. I wouldn't have huge strength in my arms, not that I'd be a Soviet weightlifter anyway, and that first year I was careful about having a drink – we lost the county final and I was good, but probably overdid it the following day and gave myself a fright. I'd be a bit paranoid if that happened, but I'd also try to enjoy life.

That sounds like a terrible cliché but it's true. You wouldn't worry about things as much. You have to strike a balance. That was a bubble I was in for a while but I'm fine now. I don't even take a tablet now, I just have a check-up once a year.

I was always relaxed enough, anyway, and the whole experience showed me what's important, certainly. It never bothered me to have time on my own. If Dawn and the girls were dancing I'd have no problem heading off on my own for coffee. And that summer, if I was off cycling or swimming on my own, I didn't spend the time thinking, 'Ah, why did that happen to poor me?' I got on with it.

The soreness I could deal with but I hated being sick. That was what bothered me, but it didn't make me pity myself, with the exception maybe of the night before the operation. My attitude was to get on with it, and get through it.

I was cleaning out the wardrobe last summer and I was rooting through the bottom of it when I came across them, my old hospital pyjamas. The memories they brought back . . . they didn't survive the cull of old gear.

Out they went into the bin.

11

WALSH PARK ON A SUMMER'S EVENING

During one of my trips back from the hospital between doses of antibiotics, Mullane called in to see how I was.

I had no money coming in: I'd only been in GSK a couple of months or so, and social welfare wasn't an option. In fairness to GSK, they'd paid me for the five weeks I was out with a brain haemorrhage, but the second time, with my heart, I wasn't there long enough for sick pay.

I think the social welfare office awarded me maybe EU19 per week. We had expenses in going to Dublin, staying overnight; I couldn't pay my mortgage again, never mind cover those.

At that point I was so sick that it barely registered with me, I had enough to do to try to get myself right, but it registered with Mullane.

He only lives a few doors up from me and he said it that

evening he dropped in.

'You can't go on like this, with no money or anything. We'll have to do something. We'll have a match.'

And in fairness to him, away they went. Tommy Shanahan, Tom Murphy, Sean Power, Sean Ormond, Liam Cusack, Michael Hogan, Kieran O'Connor, Owen Savage and a few more of them got together, and they did unbelievable work. They went out first canvassing opinion to see if there was an appetite there to support it, and then they came back to me and said there was.

Their idea was a match which would involve hurlers from Leinster and Munster, and from that basic notion the whole thing took off. It was to be called the Ken McGrath All-Star Challenge. I was in hospital and they'd update me: 'This fella wants to play, this other fella rang because he wants to play, this club in New York rang up and want to send this fella over . . .'

The goodwill was fantastic from everybody. Azzurri sponsored the jerseys, players were putting their hands up to play . . . a few weeks after the operation I went to a meeting of the committee down in the Granville Hotel and I was blown away by the detail, the attention to everything.

They organised referees, the programme, accommodation for the players who were coming down, stewards, parking . . . the operation was in the middle of April and the match was the end of June, so by the time it rolled around I was well on the road to recovery.

It was exciting. Unbelievably exciting – but it was also embarrassing, in a strange way, that there was a match being held for me. Maybe surreal is a better word, because it kept getting bigger and bigger, and I was thinking it was getting too big. Too much.

The way I rationalised it was that it could become something that could be done annually, to benefit various players, because it kept getting bigger and bigger. It was all over the press, and the focus was huge.

The day of the match I went for my walk, my rehabilitation exercise, down the new Greenway, which starts at the bottom of the hill where I live. WLR radio station rang me and asked if I was nervous about the game.

'Well, I am now,' I said. Then it hit me that I'd have to walk out in front of a fair crowd. The committee, in fairness, didn't ask me to do anything; all I was hoping was that it wouldn't lash rain.

We got down to Walsh Park early and parked in the health-care car park over the road, and the lads brought me over. The crowd started coming in, and I did a couple of interviews, and the crowd kept coming in. The players were coming into the dressing room so I went in to see them, and to thank them for making the trip.

Davy Fitz came down to manage one team, and Brian Cody was meant to manage the Leinster team, but they'd drawn with Galway in the championship so he had to drop out because they were training. Noel Skehan and Eddie Keher came down to take the Leinster team instead.

(In fairness to Brian, he rang me as I was coming in to Walsh Park. 'Sorry I couldn't make it,' he said. 'Stop, you've plenty on your mind,' I told him. But it was a lovely touch, to pick up the phone.)

And it was great from Davy. Over the years we probably had a strange enough relationship at times when he was manager, but he was one of the first to volunteer to come, to be fair.

I went into the dressing room to see them all there. It was one thing to be told by the lads who was coming, but it was another thing altogether to actually see them all there in the flesh.

I thanked them all and said a few words in both dressing rooms: I was humbled they were all there, and I told them that. I was particularly humbled because there were a few of them I'd hit over the years, and I told them that too.

A guy like Kevin Broderick, coming all the way from Galway on a Friday night. Seán Óg and John Gardiner were playing championship with their clubs that weekend, but they still came down and lined out.

Then someone stuck their head in the door: 'Did ye see the crowd out there?'

And it was gas then, to see lads who'd won All-Irelands and All-Stars and Hurler of the Year awards – they were getting nervous.

I looked out and the crowd was still coming in – streaming across the bank on the uncovered side, and filling up the stand side. The teams went out and we were asked to hold back, to walk across the field once they were out and warming up.

Walsh Park was packed. There were thousands there, and we got a standing ovation. Dawn and Ceilin got a fright – they just legged it off to the dugout. Usually they'd love the cameras, but that was too much for them. I held onto Ali's hand and we walked out onto the field together, laughing.

It was one of the greatest things that ever happened to me, or to our family. The crowd all stood and applauded, and I was thinking, 'If I put up my hand and wave they'll think I'm the Queen of England, but if I don't I'd be some ignorant clown.'

I kind of half-put my arm up. I compromised. (The players told me after that when the applause went up they looked around, and the warm-up went up fifty per cent in intensity straightaway.)

It was a lovely feeling there, though. The atmosphere was great. I had always wanted to play in a county final with Ali as a mascot, but we'd never made it back to the final after 2007; that was a lot better, walking her across the field like that.

Looking around, I realised there were plenty of fellas there I'd fought with, I'd hit, I'd argued with, but still they'd come in and paid their tenner to support us. Clubs and teams we'd be rivals with, but they rowed in behind the game.

And the game was great crack, too. One of my favourite players as a kid, either watching or playing against, Ciarán Carey, was there – he told Mark Foley he wouldn't miss it. James Ryan, another Limerick man, was there. He'd just decided to come along, though they were playing on the Sunday; he had a pint of water with us in the club. Eoin Kelly was playing for Tipperary, he just didn't want his name mentioned because he didn't want to be looking for publicity. That's Eoin for you.

The game was good crack, enjoyable for the supporters. It rained a bit during the presentations, but nothing could dampen the atmosphere, really.

I'd love to have played in a game like that myself, and I think the GAA should organise more games like that. I made that point to the Gaelic Players Association – who were very, very good to me at that time. Siobhan Earley, Dessie Farrell, Sean Potts – they were all hugely supportive.

Now, it hasn't taken off like that, the idea I had about a kind of testimonial game to help players who were finishing off, but it still might. I'd be hopeful.

After the game I must have signed a thousand autographs, and so did all the players. They were all fantastically accommodating to anyone who wanted a picture or a signature.

Mount Sion was like Woodstock. There were marquees all around, video screens, interviews with fellas, bands. A busload of lads came down from GSK, which was brilliant: I'd only been out there a few months, after all.

The night went on and on. I had a bottle of Heineken I nursed for the duration, and it must have been hard on five in the morning when myself and Dawn finally left. All the stars mixed in; it was one of the best nights I've ever had. (I remember Ollie Moran and Eamonn Corcoran were still going strong at that stage; we had a rush of blood on an All-Star trip one time, the three of us, and jumped in a hotel swimming pool fully clothed; pity we didn't organise towels beforehand, but you can't think of everything.)

I had to go up to RTE that night, a Saturday, so I needed some rest, but the place was still rocking when we left. Tony was there, Murray's big curly head, bouncing up and down.

We strolled down the hill from the club and I said to Dawn, 'That was mad, wasn't it?'

The birds were singing. The sun was coming up.

That's the GAA for me. I didn't expect any of that, and when it got so big I was embarrassed by it. Seeing all the people

251

row in behind it, stewards and guards and supporters and players . . . it was unbelievable.

After the match it was a bit of an anticlimax. I'd been in hospital for months, building up to this operation, getting ready for that. Then you have the operation, you're recovering – and then there's this match.

So the match becomes the focus for weeks at a time, all the time you're doing your rehabilitation – and then it's over. I went up to RTE the day after the match and came back down to Walsh Park then for Waterford versus Laois, and there had been more people at our game, which I felt bad about.

When the money came in from the match I thought about the cardio rehab I'd been doing out in Ardkeen, which had been such a fantastic help to me as I'd gotten stronger. The cardio rehab unit is on a tight budget, like every part of the HSE, so we felt rather than taking all the money, we donated money to them as a thank-you and they bought a couple of treadmills.

We had a dinner later in the Granville, a big night, for the organising committee. I couldn't thank them enough for all they did. I still can't.

12

LIFE AFTER THE STORMS

Back in 2009 myself and Brick went up on the train to Dublin one evening for a special mission. We had to jog down Kildare Street with a petition for Leinster House that was looking for university status for Waterford Institute of Technology, hundreds of students jogging with us. I had no problem doing that; Brick certainly didn't, and given the amount of time he spent as a student it was only right. The man must have a dozen Fitzgibbon Cup medals.

University status hasn't happened yet, but we hope it will. We always wanted to row in with causes that were important in Waterford. There were two kids sick in Tramore, Ryan and Ethan, and we organised a match between old Waterford hurlers and old Waterford United players, to raise funds for them. It was great crack, and a lot of work went into it.

When Davy came in as manager he was involved in the Make-A-Wish foundation, and he brought kids in to meet us at training sessions on occasion. If it helps some of the kids, great, but that's the kind of stuff that every county does. I don't claim Waterford is exceptional in doing things like that.

On the more political side, when there was a sit-in at Waterford Crystal a few of us went on a protest march as well. I wouldn't claim we were activists, really, but that was part of what was happening in the area, so it was part of what was happening to us. Why wouldn't we have gone on the march?

People come to support you, you support them. I've one jersey at home, framed up on the wall, because all the rest of them went to people, to causes, to fundraisers.

You're always aware of how privileged you are when you're playing intercounty, or you should be. We had a great time: we saw the world through hurling, travelled in style all over the country, had unforgettable experiences, fun you'd never have had otherwise. You have to be conscious, though, that there are people who are in desperate situations, who'd love to have the pressure of a match as the only thing keeping them awake at night.

All the lads would have chipped in that way. We often rolled in for training in Walsh Park and there might be half a dozen jerseys to be signed, or hurleys – you wouldn't even think about it, just sign it for whatever cause was involved. Every county team does that.

I suppose our team went through an awful lot of disappointment together, and that made us tight. And we're tight still. I'm still friendly with all of the players I lined out with, from start to finish, with Waterford: if I meet any of them on the street or at a match we stop for a chat, and it's half an hour gone.

When I came in the likes of Hartley, Feeney, Tony, they

LIFE AFTER THE STORMS

were of a similar age and they were close. Then the younger lads would be another group – a lot of them speeding in on their little boy racers from Tallow, however they made it into training. There are always groups in a team, lads of a similar age, but there weren't cliques. We had a real team.

That team spirit was strengthened by the adventures. The kind of high jinks and minor scrapes every bunch of lads gets into.

One time we were in New York, and me, Dan, Eoin and Jack Kennedy had a few drinks. The evening rolled on. Eoin got it into his head about the old sign they'd have in windows saying 'No dogs, no Irish'. He was saying it everywhere we went.

Every bar, every stop: 'No dogs, no Irish'. In a comedy club, and he was shouting it up at the comedians. At everyone.

We ended up in a cool spot in Greenwich Village, chatting away to the barmaid (apart from Eoin, who was just contributing, 'No dogs, no Irish.')

When it was time to leave we decided to call Eoin on his catchphrase: the lot of us got down on our hands and knees and barked and waddled away up the stairs. I'd often wonder what that poor barmaid made of that.

We thought we were grand, of course, but the fresh air hit us when we came out, and we were levelled.

Dan ended up getting a tattoo the same evening of Chloe, his daughter's name. A lively night.

When we were in Cape Town Tom Feeney got himself involved with a top international music group, but we only found out the details years later.

Peter Kirwan was the team physio for years and he had his own private practice out at his house. In the waiting room he had magazines for people, and one day one of the lads picked one up, *Hello!* or *RSVP* or whatever, when he went to Kirwan for a rub.

And there on the front was Blue, the pop group, on a photo shoot in South Africa – and behind them, as clear as day, Tom Feeney with his customary cowboy hat and rucksack (filled with water bottles and sun cream, no doubt). Blue and Tom Feeney. A winning combination.

Out in South Africa on that same trip we landed into another happening spot one evening, a bar overlooking the Cape itself. A beautiful cafe, where the trendy South African lads roll up in the convertible with the top down, showing off the muscles and the tan, the girls are dressed like models, everybody at their best . . . and us.

Someone got the bright idea that 'Sean South of Garry-owen' would be a great addition to the entertainment, so we struck it up.

It was some picture: these massive South African fellas bulging with muscles, designer gear, the girls dressed like they were going to Ascot, and a bunch of drunken Irishmen, tops off and nice little beer bellies jiggling, singing 'It was on a stormy New Year's Eve as the shades of light came down . . .'

You wouldn't have thought nudity was an Irish sports trademark, but we were partial to getting the clothes off. On an All-Star trip to Arizona we went to a nightclub one evening where they had a jacuzzi, for some reason, in the middle of the dance floor. Temptation.

J.J. Delaney gave me a nudge when we saw it.

'Come on Mac, we'll give it a go.'

Off with the clothes down to the boxer shorts, into the jacuzzi. Great lads.

Got out. No towels.

We ended up trying to dry ourselves with our socks, which meant we were strolling the dance floor half-soaked, shoes on but no socks (a long time before that was trendy). We had to take our tops off because they were soaked, too. Out of solidarity the other lads took their tops off, so there were a lot of pale grey tummies on show at the back of the dance floor.

The DJ stopped the music: 'Hey, will the *real* white guys down there please put their clothes back on? Please?'

He only had to ask us about three times.

On the same trip we ended up in Las Vegas. Feeling seedy. Found a little spot with sawdust on the floor, a long way from the Bellagio and these spots; it was more like Mullinavat than the MGM Grand. Mullinavegas, maybe.

We were staying in the New York, New York resort so the last day we hit the bar, myself and Tony. Our attitude was simple: we're on holidays, we're on holidays, and when we're back there's no going out for months. Make the most of it. Tony said to me, 'Well, Holiday Harry, are we out or what?'

Out.

After a while we wanted a change of scenery, so we crossed the strip and tried the MGM Grand. The white lions, all that.

We ended up in a disco inside there, and I got separated from Tony. When I saw him across the floor he started waving me over: 'Come here, Mac, look at this.'

When I got over he had a snake by the throat. A real snake. It was draped across a guy's shoulders – adding to the atmosphere, I suppose – and Tony was squeezing its neck, getting it to open its jaws like a hand puppet.

I'd be nervous of snakes, and I'd certainly be nervous of a snake getting angrier and angrier as its neck gets squeezed . . . we said thanks to the man with the snake and headed off before he decided to let the snake retaliate.

The same trip to Vegas, we got a helicopter ride out to the Grand Canyon. Six Waterford lads and a pilot. We were taking in the view when Mullane started imitating the traffic reports on WLR back at home: 'Light enough on the way down over the bridge . . .'

The rest of us crying with laughter. God knows what the poor pilot made of it, but at least he got us back on the ground safe and sound.

Silly things, but the crack you'd get out of it: getting wrapped up in toilet paper out in Singapore. One of the lads getting his mouth stuck to a bar counter made of ice on the same day.

The Kilkenny lads were good crack on those trips. People might think they're quiet or dour but on those trips they could let the hair down with the best of them – Tommy, Henry, they all joined in. They reminded me a lot of the old Mount Sion crowd: very serious about the game and about winning, but nuts then afterwards. Derek Lyng, Martin Comerford and Eddie Brennan were great company, so was John Hoyne.

But none of them had a disagreement with an escalator, like J.J. did when we were in Singapore.

We were all heading to a disco, but you had to go up an escalator first, so Dawn and I were waiting our turn when there was a chap carried past us on a stretcher.

I said I thought he looked a lot like J.J. Delaney, and then he saw me.

'I'm grand, Ken, tell them I'm grand, there's nothing wrong with me . . .'

It was J.J.: he'd fallen down the escalator and cut his face. They put his neck in a brace as a precaution.

'Ah, I think you'd better bring this poor man off to hospital,' I said to the ambulance men, and off they went. He was back to us within an hour.

While we were out there the Waterford lads met up with Martin Cullen, the Waterford TD, who was a minister at the time; he was out there on government business. We met him in this hotel that must have been seven-star; it was unreal, and Tom Murphy, the car dealer from home, was there as well.

Tom said he'd get us a drink; we ordered a Singapore Sling each, a long way from the top of the town, and the round must have been nearly two hundred dollars. And as we were drinking there were exotic birds flying around, because there was a bird sanctuary in the actual hotel. Surreal.

Not always intercounty stuff either: with Mount Sion we played Roanmore in a county semi-final in 1998 and we ended up giving them a wicked beating. We won by nineteen or twenty points.

As we were coming off the field there was a shemozzle in the tunnel. The old tunnel in Walsh Park: if those walls could talk . . .

Anyway, when it calmed down, myself, Roy and Eoin had all been cut and had to go to Ardkeen for stitches afterwards. A roasting hot Sunday night, waiting for the needle and thread, and the nurse takes the details.

'Name?'
'Roy McGrath, 12 Hawthorn Drive, Hillview.'
'Name?'
'Ken McGrath, 12 Hawthorn Drive, Hillview.'
She came to Eoin: 'Don't tell me.'
Back to the club, big cheer when we came in. The McGraths.

On a previous trip we hadn't done so well with Irish administration. In Argentina myself and Eamonn Corcoran had an unforgettable, and certainly unrepeatable, couple of nights out, but we also visited the residence of the Irish Ambassador, the entire All-Star party.

There's a reason those Ferrero Rocher ads were so luxurious. Butlers and servants, the best of food, all the drink you wanted, a beautiful balmy evening . . . like a movie. Perfect. The champagne came out. Happy days.

Unfortunately, none of us was used to champagne. We thought we were fine but the evidence was strongly to the contrary. Tommy Dunne was the captain, and the spokesman for the group, if you like, and he had to tell us to calm down. There were empty champagne bottles bobbing up and down in a fountain, fellas were popping the corks, singing . . .

I don't think one player managed to go out that night. The bubbly was too much, the way it caught up with us. All in bed at nine o'clock.

Sometimes the All-Star night itself posed a few problems.

The first night Eoin got a nomination was in 2007, and we all went up in a car together, and I offered him a big brother's advice.

'Use your head now, Eoin. Pace yourself. Don't be letting

yourself down. Take your time, because it's a long night . . .'

Plenty of that, all of it helpful, from Waterford to Dublin. A long time to be listening to advice.

After the presentations we went out into the bar area, myself and Tony, and we started the night off with a glass of wine. Not the usual, but going down nicely. Another glass? Why not? Another glass.

The two of us and Liz Howard, who used to be a pundit on *The Sunday Game,* having great crack.

And then I woke up on Saturday morning.

'What's . . . what's the story?'

Dawn told me what had happened. The wine had been a bad idea, because I'd fallen asleep. I'd been carried out through everyone, feet trailing on the floor, Dawn behind me shaking her head. I couldn't remember a thing: she tucked me in and headed back down for the night.

You've to go down in the morning and get your photograph taken as an entire All-Star team. I don't look pretty in that shot. Neither does Tony.

On the way there I bumped into Tomás Ó Sé from Kerry.

'Oh Jesus here's the man,' said Tomás.

'What?'

'Don't you remember what you did last night?' said Tomás, the big innocent Kerry face on him.

'I can't remember anything,' I said, heart sinking.

'Ah Ken, you gave that Dublin chap a desperate headbutt.'

I nearly collapsed. Sick as a pig and I'd done something like that I couldn't even remember . . .

Then I noticed the laughing, of course. Dawn had him prepared, and he couldn't hold it in.

And of course, all I got from Eoin on the spin home: 'Ah,

here's steady Eddie. Don't overdo it, now. It's a long night. Use your head, Eoin. Pace yourself, Eoin . . .'

It was a long drive back to Waterford.

Nowadays things are different, obviously.

I'm managing the Mount Sion senior hurlers. I love it and I know how hard it is, and it's certainly given me an insight into how Justin and Davy and all of those managers and selectors felt when they were dealing with us. And a lot of sympathy.

The buck stops with the manager. I love the coaching side of things, as many managers do, but there are an awful lot of other things floating around that land in the manager's inbox.

Mount Sion is in transition, too. It's tougher than it was; we haven't won a county title in ten years, which is a lifetime for us, but it also means we're lacking a bit of experience. Only two or three of our lads have county medals, so we only have those two or three to bring the others through.

We have good kids coming through, we're confident that some of them will help us turn the tide, but it'll take time. If I didn't think the current group had the makings of a county-winning side I wouldn't be there with them; I had a lot of offers from other clubs, but there was no way I'd manage against Mount Sion.

I had some intercounty experience, after all. Not long after my experience locking up after the Waterford lads in Carriganore – and waiting until they left the car park so I could cycle home – I got a couple of phone calls from those same players. The season had started badly and they wanted to shake things up; they wanted to know if I'd fall in and help with the coaching of the Waterford team.

I spoke about it with my father, with Dawn, and they backed me. I went in with Seán Cullinane as a selector, we joined Michael Ryan, who was managing the team, and we gave it a right go: it was spring 2012.

We beat Galway in a league game and then Dublin, to maintain our position in Division One, so we hit the ground running.

I loved it. You're dealing with high-quality players, dedicated athletes. They're keen to improve, committed to what they're doing; coaching them is enjoyable.

But when there was a lull in the intercounty scene and they went back to the clubs I saw the other side of the scene: three or four weeks of lads playing hurling and football for the clubs, and it's tougher to keep the players who are available to you interested in what you're doing.

It can be tricky: some of the players are fellas you've togged off with for years, and then you're giving instructions and telling them what to do . . . my attitude was that they were the ones asking me to get involved, so I wanted to do a proper job, particularly for Waterford.

There were one or two players who might have felt, because we'd spent so long in the trenches together, that they could say whatever they wanted at training and so on, but it's work at the end of the day. You only have so much time to get the preparation done, the physical work, the skills . . . there was a bit of mouthing one day at a session and I sent a player home, and that was the end of that.

We had Clare in the championship and there was a lack of respect, I felt, for what we were doing and for Mick as a manager in the media and elsewhere, but I was confident that we had our work done. We had a good training camp down in Fota – went to the greyhound racing one day, which the lads enjoyed – and were well prepared.

What I wasn't quite prepared for, however, was picking the team. I still find that hard with Mount Sion, but it was very tricky with Waterford. We didn't start Tony, for instance, and he didn't take it well. At all.

At the time we'd agreed that the three of us would tell him together – none of us wanted to be seen to be chickening out, particularly me: we've been friends for years and years.

We went with Richie Foley instead of Tony and he disagreed, but he wasn't over the top; he didn't bring training down or anything. He showed his class by putting down four or five weeks of unbelievable training and he more than deserved his place for the Munster final against Tipperary.

He picked up Pa Bourke that day, who'd been very good for Tipp all year, and held him scoreless. Twenty years after captaining the Waterford U21s to the All-Ireland. That's Tony Browne. That was his response.

We'd lost to Tipp by seven goals in the previous Munster final but in 2012 we were two points ahead at half-time. Maurice, Tony, Kevin Moran, Mullane – they were all going well and I thought genuinely we had every chance of winning.

Tipp got a lucky enough goal from Shane Bourke which turned it, and we lost by four or five in the end. That was an improvement on the previous season at least, we felt.

In the quarter-finals we were well prepared, we were leading Cork going into the final stages but we missed a chance to go four up – and they came back with six or seven on the trot to win. We expected to win and we were getting excited but when they came with that late burst our lads ran out of steam a little.

It was an opportunity lost in a lot of ways – I know a few of the players would have felt so, because we had Galway in the semi-final if we'd won, and we'd never lost to Galway in the championship.

There were other positives: we blooded a few good lads that season, the likes of Stephen O'Keeffe, Stephen Daniels, Philip Mahony, Gavin O'Brien.

I'm a Mount Sion man through and through, but I'm also a Waterford man; the likes of Tony and Eoin – and myself – would have a *gra* for Waterford that some players mightn't, and we'd always be keen to do the best for the county. I'd be down if Waterford lose, while some of my pals mightn't be.

Some of that might date back to our team and how well it did. The team peaked in 2007, probably, and it was up and down after that, people could take it or leave it, and the recession didn't help, but I think it's coming back, certainly.

That experience of being with Waterford in 2012 must have turned my head because I made one last burst to go back playing in 2013, but I never got going at all. Couldn't run, and earned myself yet another operation that January.

But I fell in with Mount Sion as a trainer when Anthony Kirwan, who was manager, was looking for a hand, and loved it. We got to a county semi-final and were four points up against Passage with a few minutes left, only to lose to them – and they went on to win the county title that year.

With the club the big challenge is to get fellas to believe that there's something there for them; our problem now is that a lot of the players don't really believe at times that they can do it. Last year's championship we hit twenty wides against Ballygunner; a bit of steadiness and we'd have won that. There are enough young players there to drive that on if we can just turn a corner.

We have one of the best youngsters in the country in Austin Gleeson, and the rest look up to him; it's great to have him as a figurehead for the club and for Waterford, as an ambassador.

There'd be people in Waterford who'd be happy to see Mount Sion in decline, but if you win thirty-six county titles you attract a bit of jealousy. The area is an older part of the city; the feeder school is an inner-city school where the hurling mightn't be as strong any more, so like a lot of clubs we have our hands full. That's a familiar story all over the country – in Cork, in Limerick – so the big challenge is to keep it going.

I love going up there still. It might be turning the hair a bit grey, but you can't abandon it. Nobody gives up on their club.

We can take it. We won't be down forever. We're Mount Sion.

The game nowadays isn't the game I played. I see that. At times it looks different to the game I've been playing and watching for so long. I got a taste of that when Davy came in as Waterford manager and he and the selectors picked up on my hitting a ball downfield first-time.

Chatting to an old opponent, Ollie Moran, he was saying he's all for the evolution of the game – but only if it improves the game, which is the key thing. In preparing teams you can't sit still, you have to keep moving with what's being done, but at times I feel if you say 'I didn't enjoy watching that game' or worse, 'that's not how we played', you're made to feel a bit old-fashioned, or out of touch.

But there have been times in the last couple of years when I was bored watching games. How that's happened I don't know, but you can see the crowd isn't as involved or as passionate. There aren't as many goals, there isn't the same level of excitement . . . a lot of that relates to teams needing to hold possession.

The difference to our time was if you fielded the ball at centre-back you smacked it down the field, the crowd roared, an opposing defender fielded it, and he smacked it back . . . not the most scientific hurling, maybe, but definitely more enjoyable.

The personal battles have gone out to a certain extent too. I remember preparing to mark Niall McCarthy and thinking to myself, 'I've to fucking get on top of this guy today,' or Ollie Moran, or Martin Comerford: 'I've to beat him today.'

Nowadays I don't know who's marking who, or whether they know themselves. The personal element was huge when we played: Tony would often roar over at me, 'You have him now, Mac,' and I'd say the same, 'You have him,' and the crowd reacted when you were getting on top of your opponent. That's gone.

At the same time, the players now are unbelievable. Their fitness, their touch, those are incredible. The game is going through that fad at the moment and it'll change.

That doesn't mean it'll go back. The nineties were different to the eighties and so on, but one key difference is the time and analysis county sides can put into it, particularly compared to club teams. Because when the club players hear about all of that backup, all that analysis, you have to explain that you just don't have the time for coming up with fourteen different game plans: sorry about that.

It'd be great if you could do that, but club teams don't get to head to a training camp to work on puck-out plans for six hours. It doesn't happen. Not every county can do that, never mind clubs.

Hurling has a good profile now, which is great. Going back to when I started, it was regarded as a bit of a bogger sport; now you turn on the television and hurling features in television advertising, all of that.

I hope Waterford will be part of the continuing growth in hurling, and I think the current team can do that by winning an All-Ireland. I believe they can do it. And if they do, I'll be the first man out onto the field to hug them.

The first year you're retired it's a bit strange because you see lads you played with – lads who came in as kids when you were established – and you think, 'Should I be out there?' That's only natural.

But a game comes that proves to you you're a supporter again, and that's it. In 2013 Waterford lost to Kilkenny in extra time, an unbelievable, ferocious game one summer evening up in Thurles, and I was nearly in tears after it. But coming out I saw a Waterford supporter with his son, and he had his arm around him saying, 'Don't worry, don't worry . . .'

I can still see the boy's face, because I was the same myself. Absolutely sick that they'd lost, but sick because of the defeat, not because I felt I should be playing. I was a supporter again, getting lost in the flow of the game. It was a turning point for me; the wondering about decisions was over.

We had our time, and we had a great time. I hope people don't see me and the players I lined out with as being jealous or begrudging of the current Waterford side. Anything but. I know any of the lads I played with would do anything in their power to help the new lads.

I had fifteen years in the white jersey and we won Munster titles, but we didn't win an All-Ireland. We couldn't do it. It would only be pettiness and bitterness out of us if we didn't want the new lads to do it; if they win half a dozen All-Irelands I'll be delighted for them. They were the kids who came along to watch us and now they're the men: they're the lads my kids run over to after a match to get their top signed.

We had our chances and we didn't take them. I believe this team will get that chance and that they'll take it. My only fear is what we'll do when they win an All-Ireland. I'd have to tell Eoin I'm gone for a week. Or two.

I've been working with Eoin now for the last two years. He started a coffee wholesalers, Mean Bean Coffee Company – he saw the opportunity – and we deliver coffee and coffee machines to restaurants, hotels, golf courses . . .

It's my favourite job, of all the ones I've had, and God knows I've had a few. Out on the road, chatting, mixing with people. There hasn't been a day since I started that I didn't want to go in. For a man who didn't know much about coffee a few years ago I'm big into it now.

The business is growing, and that's down to Eoin. He's

a good businessman and works hard, and the company is testament to that.

The division of labour is simple – I'm on sales, and he looks after the machines and the barista training because the one time I tried to sort out a machine I nearly flooded half of Wexford. 'Gizmo' is his nickname for me – a gremlin that water doesn't agree with. We have another driver on the road now as well, Nick Mackey – another Mount Sion man – so it's great that the business is still growing.

Things are better for Dawn as well, obviously. We always did everything together, as equally as we could. I'd row in as well as I could with everything, I'd cook the dinner no problem if I came in and she was late or working, even though nobody ever mistook me for Jamie Oliver.

Because of that I was conscious, when we had the shop, that a lot more was falling on her to do. She had her own job in the bank and at the time she was studying to qualify as an Irish dancing teacher. At that stage I'd have been roaring down the phone to her about sending that five grand to Adidas and to make sure cheques didn't bounce, all of that. When things were going well it was fine, but as it got tougher she came under more and more pressure.

When the shop closed I could see that stress lift off her, but then, when I got sick, it all fell on her shoulders again. I had the easy side of that – I was in hospital, in a routine where everything is done for you and you can watch the television as your tea is being handed to you. If you didn't feel sick it'd be great, one long holiday.

For Dawn, though, she was at work all day, then she'd have to collect Ali from her parents or my parents, head out and make sure I was okay, head back and feed them, maybe head back out to see how I was going. Plus all the housework. Plus having to pay all the bills out of one wage.

She was unbelievable. What helped was that she wouldn't be someone who'd stress out, and I'd be similar. She has her own views and opinions, she likes her nights out with her pals and I'm the same, but for choice we'd head out together. We've always had that model – her parents would always have done everything together, and my parents the same.

We've been together twelve years and we only said recently how quickly it had all flown by. When we met she had Ceilin from a previous relationship, she was five then but it wasn't an issue. I was twenty-six, probably mature enough at the time. My sister had had a daughter when she was young enough herself, and I would always have wanted Caoimhe, my niece, to be treated properly in a similar situation – and she is, by Lorna's husband Stephen, a staunch Kilkenny man.

I treated Ceilin as my own, always did – she's done her leaving cert this year and she's looking forward to going to college. And we all get on – us, Ceilin's dad, Niall, and Corina, his wife. They have a daughter, Gracie, who's a year older than Ali, and they call themselves sisters. Good enough for them, good enough for us.

Dawn's family are great to us – Elaine and Keith, her brothers Keith, Eoin and Bill. They've always been a huge help to us, and very supportive. They got into hurling a bit more when I started going out with Dawn, and they'd head out to Dower's in Ballymacaw along with her uncles, Conor and Liam.

They'd go crazy watching the games out there: I went out there one day for a game with them and I couldn't hear anything for hours afterwards.

The best thing I ever did was meet Dawn. We've the same sense of humour and we can always be who we really are with each other, even if I probably wreck her head at times.

Izzy came along in October 2015. After all the trauma of the previous couple of years that was a great boost – a great way to put those tough years behind us. She's like Ali – very lively and has her own character already. It's like she has always been in the family.

I've a house full of women now. Completely outnumbered – Dawn, Ceilin, Ali and now Izzy. I haven't a chance: even in the little cave I have for watching the sport on television they burst in and watch *iCarly* or whatever's going.

There's a fair gap between them all in age – they'll keep myself and Dawn young anyway!